THE VALIANT PAPERS

The Valiant Papers

*A Guardian Angel's Efforts to
Direct the Human Heart to God*

Calvin Miller

Illustrations by Joe DeVelasco

VINE
BOOKS

Servant Publications
Ann Arbor, Michigan

Cover and inside illustrations by Joe DeVelasco
Cover design by Michael Andaloro

Vine Books is an imprint of Servant Publications especially
designed to serve Evangelical Christians.

Published by Servant Books
P.O. Box 8617
Ann Arbor, Michigan 48107

First published in 1982 by Zondervan Publishing House

Printed in the United States of America
ISBN 0-89283-391-2
88 89 90 91 92 10 9 8 7 6 5 4 3 2 1

from the Guardian Valiant
of
Cogdill Upperton

To the Committee

I STILL FIND IT HARD TO BELIEVE that of all the places on earth that I might have desired, I have managed to arrive in Cleveland. I was in Japan the last time I came here, and I cannot say that I liked it any better than America. Either place is difficult once you have known the great dwellings of our realm. My exploits in Ohio cannot be of much interest to anyone in Upperton. Still, gentlemen, it will be your duty to explore these pages. They contain the tale of Mr. J.B. Considine. In his latter years—though he did not live to be very old—he worked as a junior executive of a firm called International Investors.

He was a baby when we first met. Aren't they all? I did not then suppose his life would be of much interest to me. Yet, for the twenty-six years I knew him I was torn between compassion and revulsion. It was his value system that bothered me most. Vices not virtues claimed his interest. His friends were like him, having his same erstwhile appetites and lifestyle. They have a saying in Cleveland that birds of a feather flock together. In J.B.'s case, his feathers matched the flock.

Throughout his brief years, he seldom spoke of God and never in a complimentary fashion. He never even dreamed clean. He was Narcissus, I'm afraid. His priority was himself. Only near the end of his years did his life turn toward real truth. Unfortunately, he died shortly afterwards. The events of his final months are all recorded in this report. I must not leave you with any notion that I did not love him. I doted on him for twenty-six years. But loving him as I did, I could never motivate him to love truth supremely.

My short years here in Cleveland have taught me many things. The last time I came to earth, my client was an atheist who read much and drank little. J.B. Considine has completely reversed these values. I have found that atheists sometimes live far more thoughtfully than petty believers who drift between cocktail lounges and small amusements. J.B. has taught me that persons who never formally reject Christ can still live an indulgent life that leaves no place for him.

If you are prone to be critical of my penchant for summarizing, believe me, it is best. There is little of interest in his first twenty-five years. However, I have dealt in detail with his last year of life. I have recorded those events in the present tense just as they happened.

Frankly, I'm tired! If it is at all possible, I would like a bit of a rest before my next assignment. My last two came a bit close together. Is it wise? Should anyone be asked to endure the dull illumination of places like Cleveland and Tokyo too frequently?

I am sure that you will find this report satisfactory. If I may be of any help in clarifying any matter, you can reach me in Cogdill where I will soon be residing. I am completing these pages from the bus station in Cleveland.

Were I human, I would be troubled with the diesel odor from the huge buses. As it is, the odor is not so offensive as the delay. I am comforted but confounded. I shall have to leave the planet by way of a common bus. Since the time is at hand, I will not be negative. Still, I would have preferred to finish writing this report somewhere other than my lap.

Life is such
A shallow night
It trembles in the
Face of light.

Alleluia,
Valiant.

To the Filing Officer
of Compound X-34, Upperton
Records Depository
Control Cogdill
Document 009-75-237b—009cx10

The Summary

I SMILE NOW WHEN I THINK OF how loudly I once protested this
assignment.

I am wistful now at his passing for it is our parting. I
remember how I once longed to be the guardian of a minister
of religion. I foolishly thought a Catholic monk would have
been the posh assignment. I imagined myself following a soft-
sandaled Franciscan around a quiet, sinless monastery. But an
American businessman! They have an interesting piece of
office equipment here in Muddyscuttle (a name I sometimes
apply to this planet). The machine is called a Xerox copier and
must have been invented by an American businessman
desperate to clone his race.

J.B. Considine is but a Xerox of all his corporate acquaintances. How sad! The "brilliant" career he had planned will
soon be taken up by yet another carbon of himself. If he had any
idea he was about to die and leave this corporation, he would
be terribly troubled. While his business is small, he imagines it
strategic. He sees himself as most necessary to life here on
earth. How overdone is most self-importance.

I hope I do not appear too negative. I know heaven still looks
down on grumbling angels. Rest assured, I have not forgotten
that Daystar began his Great Insurrection by frowning and
skipping his morning Alleluias. I know that hell always grows
out of paradise gone sour. I know also that fallen angels were
once frowning angels who lived in joyous light without
smiling.

So I smile, forcing it a little sometimes, watching J.B. dream his aggressive, selfish dreams! He constantly imagines himself as the president of his company. He flits in high self-esteem through a universe of secretaries who worship him, fight to take his dictation, carry his coffee mug, light his cigars, and make over his ideas at the quiet lunches he holds on the edge of his none-too-large desk. Like Nero in a Kuppenheimer, he strokes his chin and dictates volumes of letters and memos. J.B. is a winsome bachelor whose beautiful fans applaud his executive future.

His future will be neither as executive nor as long as he now thinks. That's the problem with most businessmen. They are forever planning to succeed without any real understanding of what heaven calls success.

I cannot quote our Christ and Beloved Logos exactly, but his best advice to my charge would probably be, "What shall it profit any company climber if he gains the corporation and loses himself?" How sad that J.B.'s dreams were but reflections in a comic mirror where his own ego was but a distorted image of his self-importance.

So you can see why I am glad that my sojourn on Muddy-scuttle is nearly done. My youthful charge has now boarded the bus to begin the trip from which he cannot return. He will go much further tonight than he supposes. We entered Muddy-scuttle together and we shall make our exit together. He will "die," as they say in Cleveland, and others will mark his passing with a satin-box ritual. They will peer at him through flowers and go home to speak of how natural he looked.

Why do they speak of naturalness at a time like this? They pack their departed in roses and whisper above the organ music, "How very natural." Fortunately, neither he nor I will have to be here for the memorial services. At his funeral they will call to memory the life and works of J.B. Considine, "The Dear Departed." In this case, "The Dear Departed" has not done much that is worthy, so there will be precious little to call to mind. Even so, they will sigh above the flowery finale that he was always a "good egg." Who's to deny it? Eggs are sold by the dozen and are indistinguishable from others around them. They are easily scrambled, and once broken, they are never collectible again.

He did, however, just recently achieve something...ah, but wait! Let me take the events of his mundane life in order without jamming the end against the first. I will try to avoid my random wanderings as I summarize his first twenty-five years.

I remember my first abrupt meeting with him. I faced Cleveland with reluctance. Atmosphere always takes some getting used to. Air is a kind of thick resistance that clots the vision and sticks to spirit. It is as invisible as we are, only thick and gummy. You feel as though you are always pushing against it. I felt awkward in it, much as these earthlings would feel if they were suddenly forced to live submerged in water.

So from the light, clean freedom of Cogdill, I found myself in atmosphere, squirming to adjust to materiality. I heard an infant cry! Both the baby and I wriggled to adjust to the same new life at the same instant. We both disliked it, but he (being immature) screamed and kicked and wept.

Wept, I say.

Crying is common in this world. It does little good to ask the reason for it. Muddyscuttle is what one might call a weeping planet. Laughter can be heard here and there, but by and large, crying is more common. As people grow up, both the sound and reason for their crying changes, but it never stops. Infants do it everywhere—even in public. But by adulthood, most crying is done alone and in the dark.

J.B.—though he wasn't called that when he first got here—wailed bitterly. He shrieked, really. But they were glad for his wail. For weeping is a sign of health here on earth. Isn't that a chilling omen? Not laughter but tears is the life sign. It leaves *weeping* and *being* synonyms. And this is how it was the night our twenty-six-year relationship began.

Still, when first I saw the weeping infant, I was immediately possessive. He was wet with life fluids, ruddy and umbilical, yet I knew instantly he was mine. I resented the nurse who handled him too roughly. She scrubbed him up while he continued his infernal—if I may use such a word—wailing. In but a few moments I found my first repugnance at his materiality dissipating. I determined then and there to be the best of all guardians.

It was three days before he was named. During those days I stood in the nursery of the hospital, never leaving his crib. "It's a boy!" they said. His father passed out cigars, which were smoked to celebrate his nativity. I did not altogether understand this smoky ritual of birth. Neither did they, but they puffed and billowed with gusto. (I no longer feel it necessary to delve into the reasons behind human antics. I have discovered that most of their nuances are irrational even to themselves.)

When they finally named him, he was called Johnnie Bertram Considine. While I did not find his name lovely, I could not stem the flow of affection that I felt for him personally. I was anxious lest the slightest harm should come to him. Mine was the same unmanageable, furious love as came from Christ himself during his time on the planet. It was not as though I did not love other mortals, for I felt attracted to them all. But Johnnie Bertram was the eye of my affection.

While he was a baby, I was often troubled. I ached the night he put his hand too quickly in his father's coffee. It hurt him dreadfully, and I found myself angry that his own father had been so haphazard in caring for him. I wanted him never to go hungry. While I know we are never allowed to resent any humans, I often found gaps in my good will. His mother too often let him cry at night merely because she wished he wouldn't. And, there was a touch of hypocrisy in her motherhood. She put on good shows of affection in public, but when J.B.'s two A.M. feeding annoyed her, she would show her irritation by handling J.B. too roughly.

I discovered that I was the very first to be able to communicate with Johnnie. I found that while my spirituality could not form audible words such as humans can, I could make Johnnie smile by warm suggestions to his tiny inner

EVELASCO

person. Smiling is ever welcome on a crying planet. And when Johnnie smiled, they would gather about his crib and "tickle" him beneath his chin. They would marvel at his grin as though they had created it. But I knew, and hoped that in time Johnnie's own experience level would tell him subliminally, that I was really the one who brought his broadest smiles.

J.B. was his name, but during his first year his father began to call him "Googul," for what reason I will never be sure. During his second year they called him "Bubby." By his third it was "Sonny." But when he started to school they had settled on "J.B.," a name that stuck to him for the remainder of his twenty-six years.

Muddyscuttlers, at least in Ohio, all begin their education as kindergarteners. This is a term of German extraction that I believe means "children's garden," though I am not sure. It was about then that I began feeling Johnnie's first attempts to shut me out. Some influence I brought to bear upon him was shrugged aside. He was mischievous, and his parents were permissive. They were disciples of the new psychology that sees all forms of spanking as barbaric. Spanking—if the term be unknown to the Committee—is the procedure of inverting children and flailing their fleshy posteriors in the interest of their futures. His parents were affording him too little direction, and I began to find it hard to get through to him myself.

His parents also gave him very little spiritual direction. Guardians know the better world. But there is only one place on earth where our world is ever discussed, and that is church. The Considines never went. I should say almost never. They did take little Johnnie there at the first of his "Googul" existence. It was the season when humans baptize their little ones into the faith. Into what faith I was never sure, since the elder Considines had no faith of their own and little esteem for anyone else's. There is a popular cliche down here that rails against "pie in the sky," and Johnnie's father had long ago decided against spoon-feeding his son "skypie." This unfortunate attitude cut Johnnie off from any background of hope.

During Johnnie's seventh year, his father had a business problem that cost him his job. He became remote and irritable. During this time he began to drink more heavily than he "ought to." He was fond of saying it just this way, though he never seemed to make it clear how heavily one "ought to." Alcohol abuse and additional financial pressures caused the marriage to begin crumbling. The arguments of his parents were often so intense that little Johnnie cried himself to sleep at night.

At such moments I hovered close to my small charge, finding my intangible angelic nature so useless. Johnnie needed the comfort of touch. Angels cannot do it: let the Committee remember this weakness. It is for this reason that Christ became a man. During those long and lonely nights with my little charge I learned this truth. We cannot save what we cannot touch. It was skin that clothed Christ's eternal nature. The same flesh that made Christ touchable could also be crucified. So God in skin was sure to die. . . . Yet those who know Christ down here praise him for coming in the flesh.

What a blessing is in simple skin! What confirmation these mortals find in touching each other. Where there is touching, men grow secure and lovers delight themselves. Where there is too little touching, frightened children weep at night, and the race grieves. I can tell you when Johnnie was a little baby, I longed for one square centimeter of skin to set firmly on Johnnie's own! Without it I hovered, useless through his crying nights.

His parents' marriage crumbled. Johnnie's father began to shatter all his marriage vows. The pall of his father's restive sexual appetites seemed to stretch over Johnnie's own mind. When he was only nine he wrote a dreadful word upon the sidewalk in yellow chalk. I pled with him to think of higher words, for men too soon become their thoughts. But Daystar had his way with Johnnie far more often than I did. As he grew older, Johnnie, like his father, craved more and more all his mind imagined.

The problems in his home increased over the next few years. They were never worse than at Christmas. Mrs. Considine overspent and Mister overdrank. The result was disastrous. On Christmas morning, both of them suffered from the results of their indulgences. Christmas brought little joy to Johnnie's world. He clung to the plastic toys they bought him, hungry for any love.

Johnnie was still getting no exposure at all to the church. He had rarely gone since his baptism. With nothing bigger to believe in, he was compelled to believe in himself. Middle-class Americans either learn of Christ or they learn to survive without him. Survival is a kind of coping where men play hero to themselves. They bulldoze their way to meaning, worshiping only what they hope to become.

There is a local hero in this hemisphere who wears blue tights and a red cape and flies faster than a guardian angel— though they would say "speeding bullet." This super Scuttler is the ego extension of the man who makes it on his own. He is a great positivist who leaps tall buildings at a single bound. Most children, including Johnnie, know more about this muscled messiah than they do our Logos. He is the icon of human ego, caped and competent and Kryptonite.

The years tumbled over one another. In spite of plodding loneliness, J.B. struggled on with homemade hope. His childish fears turned in time to teenage bravado. He was not vicious as a teenager, but he was a prankster.

Through all his early years there was only one touch of spiritual hope for the boy . . . Aunt Ida, his father's sister. Ida came often to visit. In her absence the older Considines often referred to her as a fanatic, but Johnnie loved her nonetheless. Whereas his father read him fairy tales, Ida read him stories from the Bible. In his early years Johnnie mixed the stories so badly, he could never remember if Rapunzel or Rebecca was Isaac's wife. He was sure that Hansel and Gretel and Jonathan and David all played together in the Dark Forest. For J.B., life was special when his auntie was there. He always wanted her to stay longer than she did.

Ida was a Kentuckian and not so sophisticated as the Considines. But she was devout. Her whole personality was warmed by her affection for Christ, whom she knew, loved, and talked about in her own way. She was not able to bring about any real spiritual advances in Johnnie's parents, but Johnnie was able to discover in her a God that had enough skin to be credible. In fact, as J.B. could understand God at all, he attached the entire definition to Aunt Ida.

For his fourteenth birthday, she gave Johnnie a little Bible, but he could make no sense of it. Desiring to please her, he set out at once to read it, but became mired in the genealogies of Genesis and laid the book aside. He was never quite able to understand how a book so heavy with long names had ever managed to become the favorite of someone as lovable and touchable as Aunt Ida.

As he neared his sixteenth year, the course of his life was to make a radical change. His mother and daddy's guardians met me in the hall one night in the month of February. They were ready to return to Upperton. Knowing they were about to leave Muddyscuttle, I had already braced myself for what shortly transpired. On that ill-fated night, the house was ominously quiet.

I must say that I have rarely seen such glum guardians. The Logos during his sojourn here referred to humans without hope as "the lost." The term fits in so many ways. It seems to me that during their lifetimes Johnnie's parents were lost. Lost to all they were . . . to all they might have been. They were psychologically lost . . . lost to love . . . lost to destiny. But worst of all, they were lost to Christ. Having all their lives known only his absence, they were soon to discover that the very composition of their destiny was absence.

But let me not interrupt my story. I suddenly realized that the hallway was filling with smoke. Knowing that humans can stand very little of the vaporous substance, I ran to Johnnie's room and moved into his conscience. He was instantly awake. I led. Unseeing, he never knew why he followed, but follow he did, till he was safely outside. By the time he reached the front lawn he could see that the house was ablaze. The fire had begun in his parents' bedroom, so there was little hope of their rescue. Johnnie tried to rush back into the house to drag them to safety, but the flames were too intense.

Firemen found him wandering aimlessly on the front lawn of the burning house. Though he was in his teens, he was clutching tightly to a teddy bear that Aunt Ida had given him on a long-forgotten Christmas. For some reason his hands, flailing in the darkness, had touched the stuffed animal, and he had dragged it from his home, which was shortly incinerated. The bear never left his bedroom for the remainder of his life. He did have some trouble explaining it to his college fraternity, but he kept it anyway. It was to him a strong symbol of survival. It may sound strange in Upperton, but the bear became to him a kind of idol. The Bible Aunt Ida had given him perished in the fire. But not the bear she once gave him. It seemed to J.B. the bear had drawn him to life.

Grief in adolescence is a folding of the soul. Never have I seen a mortal grieve as he did. Never have I wanted anything more than to have the power of touch. But my shortcoming was soon redeemed by the kind Kentuckian. Ida was there and held him through the many hours that he waited for his parents' satin-box rituals.

Johnnie had little to move since everything was lost in the fire. He went back to Kentucky with Aunt Ida and Uncle Harvey. Uncle Harvey will need no special reference. He was not well and died shortly after J.B. arrived. He left his widow in a kind of ache which J.B. in his own grief helped to heal.

He thought to attend church with Aunt Ida, but the sermons were too long and the music too slow. He openly declared after a couple of months that church, like the Bible, was all right for Aunt Ida but not for him. My hopes for J.B.'s conversion

degenerated rapidly over the next few years. I still did my best to encourage him toward morality and straight thinking, but such items were not high on his priorities any more. His years in the college fraternity further loosened his idealism. From college he "knocked about" for a couple of years before he finished his master's degree in business. It was a mundane but typical course of university study.

Well, the preamble is concluded! I hope the Committee will not think this summary too terse. I feel I have given these years more time and detail than they deserve. So let us proceed directly to the beginning of J.B.'s twenty-fifth year. While I have summarized his early years, I am leaving my notes on the final year of his life exactly as I recorded them.

I know it sounds odd in Upperton to speak of his final year, for there are no final years.

> *Tell all the mighty ones, truth does not lie*
> *Where trumpets have sounded the news.*
> *He who is Love rules in the sky,*
> *Yet weeps before men without shoes.*

Alleluia,
Valiant

 **Friday, June 25**

B ECAUSE J.B. IS NEW TO THE FIRM, International Investors held a dinner in his honor tonight. Now, I am afraid, he is drunk! What a non-angelic word for a non-angelic state! In my eternal life I have never worked as hard at keeping anyone straight as I worked with J.B. tonight. Even before dinner I realized that he had already had too much to drink. Temperance has never appealed to J.B.; the ghost of his father lives on, I'm afraid. Every time J.B. went back to the bar, I urged him away. It was useless. His social aggression grew with every martini. By nine o'clock he had a fearsome chemical courage toward everyone of the opposite sex.

Three times he tried to set up a "comfy session" at his apartment after dinner. Thankfully, none of those whom he propositioned were open to his suggestions. While his intentions were not honorable, they are customary in Cleveland. The base things he held in mind would beggar the fallen angels. All evening I rehearsed my lost dream of being guardian to a monk!

Here is a little list of his misdemeanors for a mere two hours:

6:00 P.M.—He purchased an unsavory magazine from a newsstand. I'm not sure even the Lord High Command knows of this one!

6:15 P.M.—He used the name of the Lord High Command in a Muddyscuttle phrase.

6:20 P.M.—He lusted after a girl at a crosswalk while I tried to get his mind on a business proposition. Perhaps the

Committee will object that I did not try to get his mind directly on Christ. Such a proposition is now so remote for my client that it would not be possible.

7:00 P.M.—He lusted after a picture of a girl who appeared in the magazine he bought at six o'clock. I tried to get him to read *Popular Mechanics* instead.

8:00 P.M.—He lusted after one of the secretaries at the dinner held in his honor.

This brief catalogue of his sins will illustrate for you my worst forebodings. J.B.'s all-consuming interest is my greatest fear. He is preoccupied with sex. What a three-letter spoiler is this word sex. It fills his mind constantly with images of full indulgence. He has but to view a strand of hair or a free ankle and he can build intense intrigues and fiery fantasies.

These fantasies did not begin at the party, I assure you. In the summary I could have mentioned that by the time he was fourteen he had an imagination that was adequate to spark an inferno. His wanton madness has grown ever since. He might curtail it some by taking charge of his mind. But he seldom does and so these storms of unrequited desire come only to a calm after his appetite has fed.

Usually he lives between longing and guilt. He seeks to cool the fever of his longing with sex. After his indulgence, his guilt is so grievous he can barely be cordial to those who afford him the pleasure.

And how does guilt stalk him? His fiery sexual visions are immediately replaced by a vision of Aunt Ida holding her Bible, wagging her head and shaking her finger furiously at him. At such moments he cannot even stand to look at the teddy bear he still keeps in his bedroom.

His ecstasy and guilt are born in one seething—full, yet empty—moment. To think that this reckless fiery force was given so that Adam and his mate might not be too casual in populating the empty planet! J.B. wants all of Adam's ecstasy and none of his responsibility. He has never considered sex as the work of the Divine Creator for anything as practical as "replenishing the earth." Sex is for himself. So much so that most of his consorts are not persons but commodities.

I wonder how long he can go on using women before he loves one. Will he ever come to that place where a caring love replaces the rapture of transaction? Now all sex is for himself: the geography, the time, the great orchestras that play through the muted speakers of his plush apartment! The flowers, the wine, the perfume, the softness and violence; these all serve nothing but his eager nervous system.

J.B. calls this "tea for two." But he is after the whole teapot, to consume it all for himself. At the height of his indulgence there are not two. There is only he—Narcissus, fondling his own manhood, breathing heavily over his own desirability. Pretending to be sharing, he grabs all delight and crams it into his own knapsack.

His behavior at the party was consistent with his life as a whole. I felt a comradeship in watching the other guardians there. The whole lot of us were scurrying about in an attempt to keep sin to a minimum, but it was a maximum night.

The only guardian I envied was Cloudsong. His charge is a posh assignment: a certain John MacDonald who is a tee-totaling fundamentalist. Cloudsong was a little arrogant about his client's exemplary behavior. He was the only angel who had time to sit in the corner and catch up on his report. MacDonald left at 10:30—hardly the hour that the "red-blooded" depart—and probably both he and Cloudsong were at rest before midnight. The boss confided to J.B. that MacDonald was a "Seven-Up sipper" and hence is called a fuddy-duddy throughout the company.

But whatever his reputation at International Investors, MacDonald has left Cloudsong the envy of the angels. I am about to change my mind about clerics being the easy ones. I think I would rather have a fundamentalist fuddy-duddy—especially a married fuddy-duddy. Mrs. MacDonald has a certain pinched look that must have been of some assistance to

Cloudsong: even sin needs some spark of warmth to catch fire. Though the fundamentalist MacDonald might desire to defy his guardian, he might not have the courage to go against a countenance like hers.

J.B. is across the gamut from John MacDonald. J.B. neither resists nor struggles against booze or lust. Sex and liquor can both be touched and form for him a beckoning image of what is real and good.

I am not sure that things are as they appear with John MacDonald. I know his guardian well. We once served in earth's Eastern Hemisphere together. Cloudsong knows that MacDonald is what our Logos called a hypocrite during the painful years he spent in these wallows. MacDonald's prayers have only an eighty-foot radius. His low-wattage prayer communication is as infrequent as it is weak. Religion is all theater with him.

Cloudsong told me MacDonald's only prayer ever to make it all the way to Human Petitions was the one he uttered one night when he lost control of his Pontiac on a mountain road. His prayer was urgently answered by God. Even as he plunged over a barricade, his bumper caught on a tree stump, and Upperton has not heard from him since. Cloudsong probably has no fewer problems than other guardians—they are only different in nature.

Seeing Cloudsong with his charge has left me in a quandary. I can't decide whether I had rather guard a lecher or a hypocrite. MacDonald is full of God-talk when it is convenient and when it is not. He has invited J.B. to church with him this weekend, and I can only hope J.B. will go. J.B. finds a kind of Aunt Ida fascination with MacDonald's "Holy-Roller mentality." So there is some possibility he will go, especially if he thinks he might catch sight of some "religious chickie." With this term, J.B. refers to those women Mr. MacDonald reverently calls his sisters in Jesus.

I would not leave the impression with the Committee that I believe that there are only two sins, drunkenness and lust. The great sins of every era are sociological, to be sure. Man's inhumanity to man are the great sins of genocide, racism, and unbridled power. How often has the church crusaded against booze and loose women, and never mentioned the great woes that leave humanity as refugees from hope? Still, J.B. is not so wide a thinker as to see these larger sins. His is a near-sighted hedonism that might be called the "Whiskey and Women" syndrome.

Now the party is over and I am trying not to dwell on the length of my assignment. I am taking it one day at a time. Methuselah's old guardian, Featherdraggle, used to say that no matter how tough it gets in the material realm, be grateful that God has put a limit on human existence. The whole thing will be over in seventy years. At least this is the average. I take heart in remembering that what Featherdraggle had to endure for centuries will soon be over for me.

All splendor and praise to our Lord High Command
With Nova-blue Starfire encircling His head.
He holds constellations with wounds in those hands,
Now breaking the light-years—once breaking the bread.

Alleluia,
Valiant

Monday, June 28

THINGS ARE SWEET and sour at once.

What could be better than a Muddyscuttle summer day?

Considine did go to church yesterday, but he told a friend in his carpool this morning, "I don't think I want in on this religious jag." Church offended him. Having lived through it with him, I think J.B. may be on the side of the angels.

I have been to church so seldom that I had forgotten the obscenity of some Muddyscuttle worship. I was stunned at the starkness of human praise in this particular service. The singing was more "hallelujah, brother!" than "alleluia, Father!" In one hymn Upperton became "Up yonder."

The service went like this: humans called ushers met the guests at the door to help them find a seat. I couldn't understand this, since so many were empty that no one would have had the slightest difficulty finding one. These ushers also gave worshipers a bulletin. This paper had the order of worship all printed out along with the church softball and bowling schedules for the week. It was a most unusual document. It also contained advice to pray for the sick so they could soon be back in worship. I could not escape the feeling that the sick may not want back in.

The service began as the choir entered and sang. I have heard few human choirs since I left Upperton, but I was shocked at what tonsils and adenoids do to praise. J.B., unaccustomed to anything finer, was not offended at this. After the choir sang, there was a period of general singing called "congregational hymns." J.B. had some trouble with this. They sang a hymn called "Come Thou Fount." He was a little embarrassed that he had no idea what a "fount" was, but he assumed it was because he was so irregular at church. The second verse had an entreaty to "raise an Ebenezer"; J.B. felt it must be at least as hard to sing about Ebenezers as it would be to erect one.

John MacDonald seemed to enjoy everything. Not so his guardian. My assessment of MacDonald is correct. Cloudsong continually urged MacDonald to lower the volume of his singing, for he was always louder than the rest. During the sermon Cloudsong could not keep his charge awake. The poor guardian spent the entire service seeking either to silence or to rouse his client.

During the offering J.B. put two dollars in the plate and smiled at his generosity. I tried to keep him from feeling self-righteous, but he grew smug. His religious arrogance lasted only until the man down the pew put in twenty. Then J.B. looked away and was clearly glad when the offering was over.

They had a special soloist who was listed in the bulletin as "Gloria and her Gospel Guitar." She strummed and sang the most unusual piece of music I have ever heard. The song was called "I'm just a Jesus Cowgirl on that Trail Ride to the Sky." I thought her song was satire and was really enjoying it until I noticed several around me crying from the emotional impact. *Gloria* is a favorite word in Upperton anthems, so I was expecting something a little more *in excelsis deo,* but this Gloria was not in the *excelsis* category. Brother Buford, a good Kentuckian, got up to preach. His congregation listened intently, but his dialect never translated. Nor did his message.

I'm afraid it may take a good deal of effort to get J.B. back to any church again. I was troubled by the quality of worship in that church. I do not berate the sincere. Still, I wonder how some of these poor mortals will ever stand the transition to

eternity. How shall these who worship with this sort of praise ever adjust?

When the long sermon and service had ended, the choir sang "God Be with You till We Meet Again." The implication of this chummy anthem was that he had been there all through the service.

I managed to talk with Cloudsong after the experience. He agreed that there had to be something more effective to motivate J.B. toward conversion. Cloudsong told me that there is to be a gospel telecast on Thursday. Unfortunately, it is across the network from a baseball game. There is not much chance that J.B. will miss that game . . . it is a big game. He's been talking about it and "laying money" on it for weeks.

There is a new man at work named Beau Ridley. J.B. has noticed him praying in the cafeteria before his meals. To J.B. this is an offensive and eccentric custom. Ridley has taken a position in the Corporate Investment Division of International Investors. While J.B. has already mentally labeled him a Christian of MacDonald's ilk, I earnestly hope that Ridley knows our Logos. His guardian is a certain Joymore, who appears to be consistently calm. His emotional balance is a positive quality that may appeal to J.B. Oh that J.B. would unclamp his senses and let God in!

My desire to see J.B. "saved," as MacDonald would say, is not based upon his moral condition alone. There are many noble things about J.B.'s world view. He loves children and is even considering giving some of his Saturday time to working in a boys' organization in a deprived section of inner Cleveland. He is courteous to a fault. He goes out of his way to show little courtesies to all he meets. He is generous in most every expression of his life. As I said earlier, he doesn't think much about the great injustices of the planet. But were he to discover them, I assure you, he would grieve over every inhumanity to man. He just hasn't looked beyond the narrow limits of his current world.

Still, he must be reclaimed, for Daystar's chamber is forever. I love J.B. too much to let him slip beyond the glorious destiny I have in mind for him.

Come gallant in time, you couriers of love.
Stir up in your zeal his mighty attack.
Stand mute for the day that he entered in time.
Shout songs for the day he came back.

Alleluia,
Valiant

A Certain
Wednesday
in July

I MUST HURRY J.B. DOWN THE pathway to encounter. He is so confident of time that he assumes it is endless. People do not manage time, time is the manager of most people. Life is short on Muddyscuttle. I knew an old starclerk in Cogdill who used to say, "It seems that I barely get the file folder out of the birth box before I put it back in the death box. There is nothing after that but to put it on hold for the Termination Event."

The most dreadful aspect of life on earth is its brevity. Sometimes when the wind blows across this planet, you can hear the wail of dying souls, weeping as they terminate. Only guardians hear it. Yet, it must float to the very foundations of Heaven. Life is so temporary and diminished here.

How opposite it is to life in Upperton. There being ever grows and spirits densify and enlarge. How can we guardians ever really understand pain or the curse of decaying materiality? But to consider this littleness is the real tragedy of human thinking. I constantly think of nothing else except J.B.'s need of eternal life.

Even as I squint in the dim illumination of this world—the lighting is always bad here—I carry for J.B. more brilliant hope than he can imagine.

Please, as you read this report, understand that darkness always retreats from true knowledge. Knowledge cancels darkness. It amazes me how earthlings are prone to think they know it all, yet live on this dingy planet quarreling over trifles. It is ignorance that makes the planet dark. They know so little of the truth that really matters. This certainly is true of J.B.

As their minds are dark, so are their appetites. They desire after all the wrong things. Their dark love of things must ultimately be set against the incandescence of God's reality. Consider this: they spend their years squinting over bankbooks and investments to gain but a little of the gold that paves our streets in Upperton. The treasures of this world's kings are but cobblestones in higher worlds. The prisons here are filled with those who stole only little nuggets of what is our pavement. J.B., like all the rest, is captive. His appetite for things does not compare in fervor with his lust for sex. Still, he seeks to sate both of these glistening enticements.

Let me not rail too severely on human value systems. Sexuality, unabused, is noble. I still remember my tour here in the late seventeen hundreds. There was sexual abuse and materialism then, too. But in the interim I have seen these appetites swell to a fever. Idealism has so degenerated in the race that every man is a bargain-hunter seeking great treasure at little expense. It all reminds me of what Wordsworth once wrote:

> The world is too much with us; late and soon,
> Getting and spending, we lay waste our powers.

Getting for mortals is a one-word definition of life. Having and loving is the two-word definition of what goes on down here. Oh, that life might enlarge for J.B. Once free of shopping and the bedroom, he would live in better light. While his hungers are so earthbound, he can only content himself with darkness. The light is always better when our appetites break their purely human tethers.

> *The Logos was life but they murdered him there*
> *On this planet of crosses and graves.*
> *There is treasure and light above this dark air*
> *Where life treasures trifles and raves.*

Alleluia,
Valiant

Of August and Two Television Episodes

A KIND OF HOPE occupies my attention.

On an August Sunday J.B. woke up to listen to Carlton Classie, a phenomenon in the "video church." Dr. Classie preaches with distinct diction and is always very positive about life. This Sunday he delivered a sermon entitled "The Winner." "You can be a winner if you think you are a winner," cried Dr. Classie. J.B. really liked the sermon. His eyes were glued to the TV screen. He moved only once and then in a mummified fashion to the refrigerator to get himself a can of beer.

"Remember," said Classie, "your mentality is your vitality. You can win if your mind doesn't sin. Think high, young man. Your career will soar only where your mind has already flown. God is a flags-down-throttles-open God. Low thinking will never let your career lift off the runway."

Classie went on uninterrupted. "God wants winners in this world. No loser ever honored God. God's mind is so glorious the entire universe proceeded from it. He is the Master Thinker. If you want to learn to think like God, you must think big! Take those difficulties that threaten you with defeat and wrap them in victory and give them all back to the Master Mind. Remember the airliner that flies too low is in danger—it is only safe at the heights. Most airline tragedies are not *air* tragedies. They occur on the ground. They are runway failures. Lift into the pure, clear air. There you are alone with perspective. All your little difficulties will dwindle as you gain elevation. Break the grind with a godly mind. Soar . . . Unchain your soul and take control. Soar . . . soar . . . soar!"

All too soon Dr. Classie's sermon was over. It was the first one J.B. has ever heard to its conclusion. He belched—like a common runway failure. He reached for his toothbrush just as Dr. Classie swelled gallantly and moved in close to the screen, "This is Dr. Carlton Classie reminding you to turn your pain to gain. . . . *You* can win if you think you can." The music swelled, and there were some nature photographs. J.B. belched again and turned off the set.

Television is new since my last tour. It is the monumental preoccupation of the bored. Americans watch an endless parade of video dramas until a million pointless plots have fused. They seem to have so little use for talk, so they watch—obesity with eyeballs. They eat, drink, and make merry all before the blue-dull video glare. They show little emotion unless there is a power failure. While the device is the god of secular thralldom, Dr. Classie's program is one that at least hints at Upperton.

But even TV can hold moments of glory! On Thursday, J.B. actually watched a gospel telecast. He had intended to watch a sporting event, but as it happened, there was a great deal of video "fuzz" on channel three, so baseball was out of the question. J.B. tried to eliminate the blur. He twisted the various knobs in anger. He grew angry as he tried to make the screen clearer. But clarity was not to be his. Finally in utter frustration he spun the channel selector, feeling it to be better to watch something you don't like than not to watch at all—such is the power TV has over most Americans.

At length J.B. left the stubborn, blaring television, walked to the bar, and fixed himself a highball. Channel six, where the hapless device became fixed, was coming in loud and clear. As he sat down, J.B. faced a stadium filled with people who had come to listen to a man named Frankie Williams. Before he spoke, the Conquest Choir was singing melodies about sin and eternal life. I know now I am adjusting to the planet. Perhaps I am overadjusting. I suddenly found myself listening to Frankie Williams just as if I needed what he was saying.

Best of all, J.B. actually listened to me. When he was about to mix himself a second drink, I suggested that he couldn't afford a moment away from the set. He shrugged off my initial suggestion, until I reminded him that his Aunt Ida had always admired him and would be embarrassed to know he was drinking in front of a man of God.

Williams was preaching on the Second Coming of the Logos. He preached on human drunkenness and gluttony that would exist at the end of time. At the mention of these intemperances, J.B. sucked in his stomach, covered the candy dish, and pushed his empty cocktail glass out of sight. He fidgeted in his chair. He tried to think about his Aunt Ida. Her image for him was more accessible than the abstract God that Frankie Williams preached.

Then Williams talked about the millions of businessmen in American corporations who were living for themselves. "These men," he said, "have never really considered making Christ the Lord of their lives." J.B. was actually smitten when the Conquest Choir began singing the entreaty. He was choked with emotion. I thought for a moment he was going to respond, but he suddenly turned off the television, sat down, and sighed in relief that the telecast was over.

I prodded him to read the Bible that his Aunt Ida had given him at high school graduation. He lifted it from the bookshelf, turned it over in his hand, and cautiously opened it. Haplessly he thumbed the pages to Matthew One. Why do all beginning Bible readers feel they must begin either in Matthew One or Genesis One? "No!" I screamed to his subconscious. "A thousand times no! ... You'll be right back in the 'begats' again." Soon he was reading, "Zorababel begat Abiud; and Abiud begat Eliakim."

"I must read on just like Frankie Williams said," he thought. Fighting the urge to quit, he went forward: "Eliakim begat Azor," said Aunt Ida's great gift.

"I wonder why Auntie considered this such a hot gift," he said. "She always said it would bring me comfort in a time of grief. . . . 'Azor begat Sadoc, and Sadoc begat Achim.' And what could she mean that I would find great peace in my conflict? . . . 'Eliud begat Eleazar; and Eleazar begat Matthan,'" he stopped and folded the volume.

I urged him to go forward just a little, but he would have none of it. He was utterly bewildered that Aunt Ida and Dr. Classie and Frankie Williams all found such comfort in a book so filled with "begats." He concluded them all to be a kind of third sex.

Exhausted at his attempt to read the Bible, he lay down for his nap. He might have fallen right off to sleep, but I prevented it by filling his mind with images. I kept playing pictures of his Aunt Ida at prayer across the inner screen of his thoughts. He seemed to be envisioning a change for himself. He was experiencing a destitution—the kind that might actually precede the human phenomenon of repentance. Surely his reclamation will be forthcoming.

The heart can kindle scarlet fire
When men grow wiser than desire.

Alleluia,
Valiant

The Trees

THE TREES ARE LOVELY. I am captive to the planet. This bondage fell upon me as I walked with J.B. in the park today. He sat beneath an oak tree and wondered over all the years it took to make the plant. I marveled that it grew so quickly. Oaks are somehow marvels in this topsy-turvy world where trees outlive men.

But the grove *is* grand and I have heard that in the West there are trees that were already tall when our Beloved Logos walked this earth. I see increasingly why God loved this planet so! Here the eyes may feast on nature, beholding geese set against the incendiary skies of summer evenings. There are gray mushrooms tufted in ochre grass. J.B. studied a ladybug that walked a spotted-amber promenade upon a linden twig. Does it seem incongruous that angelic eyes would gaze upon an orange insect in admiration for the jewel-like precision of God's meticulous detail?

I'm glad J.B. does love nature. But I wonder that he cares so little about nature's Maker. J.B. is evidence that creation may stop men short of the Creator. They fondle the art, content never to know the Artist. They see a tree and marvel at its beauty, but never go on to ask about the Maker of trees.

So J.B. does not suspect that his awe is only pantheism. He clings so desperately to this world, it blinds him to the world to come. His love for verdant towers and leafy shrines keeps his worship low. This leaves both his life and destiny earthbound.

Life for J.B. is all sensual. If he cannot see it, smell it, or touch it, it holds no value for him. He walks by all extrasensual reality never suspecting its existence. This leaves his world immediate and ours remote. The martyrs could not afford the luxury of J.B.'s pantheism. They longed for Upperton, for they were about to lose this present world. But in Ohio there are few dangers, so people adore creation without giving the Creator a thought.

But I am fickle.

Just when I want to criticize J.B.'s intrigue with the out-of-doors, I become fascinated with a swan moving silently across a pond. September is magnificent and must deserve some little Alleluia. Lest you think I have been distracted from my task by nature, let me assure you my motives are unchanged. I spend every hour now in hope of my client's conversion.

It is true that I did not fare well in getting him to read his Bible, but I am learning to take one step at a time. I regret that it is forbidden for guardians to have the knowledge of when or if reclamation will occur. Without this information, I remain troubled by the certain event of his termination, which date I do know. There are only a few more months till his satin-box ritual.

I sometimes rebuke myself, feeling that I have become too familiar with Considine. I need to remember that I am his guardian, not his "chum." I realized too late that I almost considered our trip to church or our carpool conversations as outings for the both of us. Today our aloneness with the trees was almost rapturous. I was prone to view the telecast with J.B. as a sort of "lovely evening at home." I know I am not on Muddyscuttle upon some sort of interplanetary lark. Time itself concerns me only when I remember it is of utmost importance to him. I have all the time in the world, but J.B. will shortly run out of it. I must force myself to remember Raphael's Code, to which I first subscribed my allegiance to Upperton:

I, Valiant, in the name and authority of the Lord High Command do swear to the Beloved Logos, Ruler of spirit

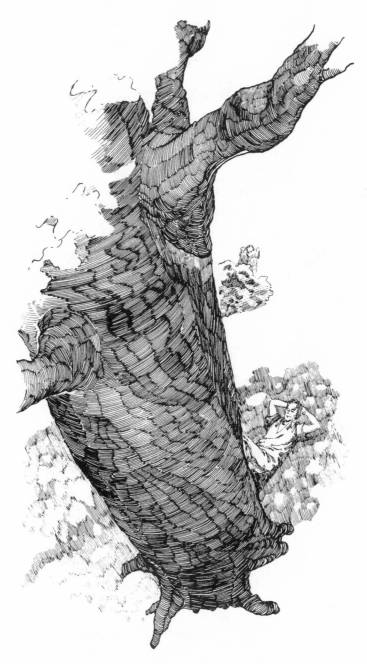

and matter, this twofold commission of his Majesty, the only true Sovereign and source of being. First, I shall do all within my power to work with human willfulness so that no unclaimed spirit ever shall be lost in Daystar's prison house of fire. Second, I will guard the physical life of my charge so he may acquire unending life and come with all Upperton to adore the Logos.

It is an unfortunate tendency of most guardians to seek friendship with their clients. While I am generally doing the right things, I wonder if I am always doing them for the right reasons.

I am spellbound by Frankie Williams. He certainly seems a good ambassador of Heaven. With every Conquest, thousands more come to know Christ. But the Logos never liberates by thousands. He always liberates one person at a time. May J.B. see that eternal life—however it looks on telecasts—is an individual affair.

I no longer feel any envy over Cloudsong's assignment. MacDonald speaks of Christ, but he seems so much in love with himself and his need for recognition. How easily religion may sour! For MacDonald, the church is a miracle show where one may speak of God, yet glory in his own importance. MacDonald really thinks God has joined *his* team, content for MacDonald to be the lucky captain.

MacDonald grieves because J.B. is "unsaved," and yet Cloudsong grieves because MacDonald is "too much saved." MacDonald's view of the Logos makes God a great "grinch" who lords it over humankind for the sheer joy of slapping hands.

It is such a long way between what J.B. is and what MacDonald would like him to become. MacDonald would like for J.B. to be a Christian rather like himself, since he considers his own faith to be the standard of the planet. If MacDonald could only get one glimpse of J.B. sitting in his underclothes with a can of beer in his hand, smoking cigarettes, he would think it impossible for him ever to attain the same level of sainthood which he himself has achieved. As MacDonald sees it, God will drub a man to hell for parlor games, tobacco, or wine.

MacDonald has been in constant misery since his reclamation. He suffers from either the guilt of sins which he's committed or the gnawing fear that he may soon fall into a major sin of some sort. Guilt is a violence that obscures God with an egotistic inner focus that produces nothing of value. Guilt steeps the soul in passionate self-concern.

Joymore, an old acquaintance of mine, is the guardian of Beau Ridley, the new man in the company. Ridley is pleasant and forceful, and J.B. is drawn to his charm and wit. J.B. has now come to know him and is no longer as critical of Beau as he once was. Most of J.B.'s judgments are *a priori* and therefore, much of the time, wrong. Except for Beau's habit of saying grace in the company cafeteria, which still offends J.B., he seems both comfortable and authentic.

As J.B. is drawn to Beau, I also am drawn to his guardian. I only hope that J.B. and Beau might become friends. This would permit Joymore and me to deepen our acquaintance. I used to visit with him regularly several anguria before the humanization of the Logos. A new friendship with someone from home might permit me to escape the earth fever that has captured me of late.

I am an angel in doubt. Maybe it's because my time is short, but my fascination with this planet pervades my whole world view. I must be honest. I do love the world where I serve. I sometimes grieve that it is all destined for fiery erasure at Operation Clockstop. I must redouble my efforts at protecting my charge, lest the ancient fire fall upon him unaware.

He is glorious evermore
Who holds both love and fire in store.

Alleluia,
Valiant

From a Bedroom on an Autumn Night

J.B.'S SECURITY IS MY PASSION. How shall I really protect my client in such an unpredictable world? There are many things over which I have too little control. The air tragedy on Thursday last is one example of what I mean. What if J.B. had been on that plane? All 119 Muddyscuttlers were "lost," as they say down here. On the same plane there were 119 guardians, never mentioned by the press. It is just as well. None of the guardians could do a thing to avert the disaster.

The fault lies in protoplasm, which is hardly worth its carbon formula. If human flesh warms over a mere 108 degrees, it succumbs to fever, the mind fries, and life is gone. If the temperature lowers to 90 degrees, the body chills and dies. Mine is the task of keeping my fragile human client between these stingy temperatures until he can be reclaimed. I must make his every tragedy a triumph. In every mishap, J.B. must be a "survivor." His hope of Upperton means he must remain in the flesh. Flesh? What is it? Nothing more than the sinew of dust! What can be said for it? Weather stings it. Sharp objects puncture it. Disease infects it. Old age alone will crack and consume it. Wars liquidate it.

Human beings seem to willfully complicate our work—it is as if they are eager to kill themselves. They assassinate, murder, and declare war. How can we possibly help them stay safe while they dream up a ghastly arsenal of ideas to kill themselves? They dare to set flesh against gunpowder and nuclear fission and war. Nineteen million men die every century from such scourges.

I often think of the way all life hurries toward death here. Twenty thousand died in an earthquake, and the number of small disasters are manifold. I could go on to speak of such human foibles as the Hindenburg or the Titanic. Specific instances matter not. The point is that again and again, Muddyscuttlers perish by the score while a host of guardians watch and weep. Our power over human safety seems an unending and fruitless vigil.

Even when protoplasm survives, it still says little about the quality of life. It is here I suffer my worst feelings of unrequited hope. How I wish J.B., who has little left in the quantity of his life, might yet discover a real quality of life.

Has his life any quality? What I must now report will be displeasing. I have suffered a setback. While J.B. was "having a few" at the Mayflower Lounge last night, he met Cassie, a youthful and coquettish human.

Cassie's guardian is an old angel named Alphalite who first served as a guardian of a Hittite princess before the Lord High Command ever initiated the writing of the Bible. Alphalite knows Featherdraggle and said they once roomed together in Upperton before the humanization of our Logos. Alphalite's Cassie is as independent as my client. She, too, pursues her own desires. They both see themselves as liberated, but it is a liberation that is about to destroy them. All of J.B.'s outer offenses proceed from his inner self. His mind is the real culprit in his physical gluttony. J.B.'s actual indulgence is but the performance his prior thoughts rehearse. As goes the gray matter, so goes the man. If he would only think higher, he could live higher.

Alphalite seems less concerned about Cassie than I do about J.B. Since he was once the guardian of a Hittite princess, Cassie must seem tame to him. Oh, if I were as old and wise as he! I know I am suffering from a lack of experience.

I know that my client's behavior with Cassie is much the product of something that angels never can understand—

procreation. We guardians came directly from the foundries of the Spirit. Adam and Eve were the first humans to arrive directly at being. Since them, people have been participating in the process of making people. I know, too, that lust is the mechanism that drives this human part of the divine plan. Thus for humanity to survive, the High Command had to endow it with the forces of sexuality. If I did not know how perfect the Creator is, I might believe he overdid it all. Well, let me get on with the story!

It pains me to have to tell you that J.B. brought Cassie to his apartment . . . and the whole episode was most embarrassing to Alphalite and myself. Two humans making love and two angels looking away, wishing for them better value systems. Not that I haven't suffered through this with J.B. a hundred times before. But I felt he was making such good progress.

Nevertheless, nothing would dissuade him. I tried to help him think of the Frankie Williams telecast. His intentions rushed forward. Even my suggestions of Aunt Ida's broken faith in him would not avail. Had they been man and wife, Alphalite and I would have found the situation a fond and close expression of noble eros. But what is to be said? We must regard the whole affair as but a gluttony of glands: a bogus offering of soul.

What shall I do? The same sentiment my client calls love, the Bible labels lust. If J.B. and Cassie could know real love, they would be slow to label their appetites with such grand words. I grieved to give the night to Daystar, but his will became their burning fever once again. Reason is on God's side while the ꞏ voltage of human experience remains on the side of evil.

The planet is crazy about this phenomenon of sex. "Sex" is so short a word, it scarcely makes three letters. SEX, SEX, SEX. It must be said three times to make three syllables. Yet, this silent, screaming, inner drive drives all! The entire course of history pivots on this passion.

The entire planet celebrates one common appetite. The admen make every possible use of this omnipresent urge. Sex sells soap and autos, hand cream and clothing. From highway billboards half-naked forms, gargantuan in size, gaze out over eighteen lanes of traffic. The titan nudes smile down in bronze skin to sell the products they espouse. Seductive mouths smile with an intrigue across the void, begging tourists to lust, if only for an instant, as they hurtle down the freeways.

J.B. and Cassie are like their world. It is natural to the both of them to "make love," as they say. They make nothing really but tangled psychologies they shall spend the rest of their lives unraveling. What they experience was created in Eden by a lavish Artist, who thought in all his creativity to give the race the gift of intimacy. So to Adam and Eve was given the grand donation—the simple pleasure of skin. It was a tiny ecstasy compared with that great cosmic love the angels know firsthand. But these who never know the best will exalt the least. This great tactile pleasure is the planetary preoccupation.

What shallow occupations Daystar gives the globe! They follow their passions until the fever in their systems leaves them powerless to control the firestorms of their indulgence. The megavoltage of their eros burns hot till passion electrocutes itself and slumps in weak relief. Then they lie quietly, contented in the smoldering aftermath and speak of it as "love" which they are "in" or, indeed, have "made."

Their strange and fiery ritual was over in a furious quarter hour. J.B. had a certain inner knowledge that ecstasy wasn't his by right. But neither of them speak of rightness or wrongness in their relationship. They boast of their liberation from the older, other times. They even then turn on the lights to show how liberated they are. They smoke in bed and speak of their enlightened innocence. They marvel that they feel joy without shame. "We are Aquarian," they said when they had finished. They are strange Aquarians who refresh themselves from fetid jars, yet call the water clean.

I will not have the Committee think that I believe that their illicit pastime is the greatest of all sins. No, the world bleeds from much greater kinds of moral and social wounds than J.B. and Cassie create. But their own indulgence blinds them to any greater purpose for themselves. Further, they confuse their pursuit of pleasure with the pursuit of happiness.

Oh, that they knew what Alphalite and I have dreamed for them! If they could only see the Christ reaching in wounds to receive them, they would cry for honest love. They need the wisdom of Christ to understand what it really means to be liberated. Christ cried during his humanization that people should not call liberty by lesser names, for self-denial is the only pier upon which real love rests. Commitment is the only basis of true love. Love that will not commit itself is at last only lust. J.B. calls his lust love, for it allows him to gratify his flesh without obligating himself. J.B. and Cassie are not lovers, only lusters. They misuse each other and name the misuse love.

Human intimacy is not wrong. It is the very gift of the High Command to all who dwell upon this planet. But even when it is right, chief of virtues it can never be. The highest love does not seek sweating starbursts. Neither J.B. nor Cassie can admit this without their self-respect crumbling. Inwardly they know that there must be a higher love that does not come wrapped only in petty ecstasy. The best love still comes back from hilltops with wounded hands, forgiving its assassins.

I remember well the day Christ died. The vultures circled the gallows, but he would not leave the world. He hung there just as if he had to do it. He would not abandon those puny nails and come home. Finally his heart broke, and they laid his body firm against his mother's coarse-cloth garment. She cried. All Upperton agreed in anguish.

We waited through the hours with drawn swords, but he would not give the word. We knew he wouldn't. God's Beloved was in love! Christ was IN LOVE with a fallen planet, whose answer to love was the gallows.

How shall I communicate such excellence to J.B., whose definition of love is only penny-ante?

Call dying love.
Call flesh pretense.
Call human ecstasy a fault.
Call Heaven's love, all moral sense.

Alleluia,
Valiant

The Last of October

THE LOVERS HAVE NOW SPENT two weekends together and seem to be settling into a lifestyle. I was wrong about Alphalite: he feels that the Hittite princess was "chaste" compared with Cassie. The princess, he says, always sacrificed doves to atone for her promiscuity. Cassie feels no such religious duty.

J.B. and Cassie have a pattern of behavior that is predictable. After work on Friday they begin drinking to loosen up. They are usually quite loose before they leave the lounge. Once they begin these sessions, it is most difficult to bring angelic influence to bear. I even feel sorry for them. Their naivete contains a nobility of spirit, but one that is tightly chained to their frailties.

Once J.B. brandies his brain, I have trouble communicating with him. As I said earlier, it is in his mind that J.B. loses the battle. He swims in fanciful fornication for an entire afternoon before his actual indulgence. I myself swim in his fantasies, shouting idealisms over the roar of his glandular cascade.

I am weary these days. My one refreshing thought is that I am spirit and never shall be subject to mortality. Homesickness—that's what it is! I've only a few months to go here and then I shall be home again. How much I would give to know that when I enter Upperton, J.B. will be with me.

J.B.'s favorite sins always grow in acceptance till at last he blesses them. He has split himself into two people. One is a monk and the other a seething bohemian. The two wear the very same wardrobe yet never meet, so there is never any conflict. It is a safe arrangement by which many here on earth manage a double life that appears single in each of its contexts.

I heard of a poor man in France who many years ago was compelled by the state to be an executioner. The first time that his trembling hands raised the bloody blade of the guillotine, he cried, trembled, and wept that he was man. He could not bear to hear the victim screaming and kicking in protesting those who dragged him forward and clamped his straining form in the braces. He closed his ears against the dull thump and turned from the tense neck that lay against gory steel. So it was with the first dozen. Soon, however, he freed himself to look. Then he gazed. At last he rose eagerly on those mornings when the executions were scheduled.

The mind will soon permit what it earlier abhorred. I remember the first time that J.B. indulged in illicit sexuality. He was morose for days. Images of Aunt Ida dogged his guilt. He could scarcely eat, he felt so bad. Soon he tolerated his sin. Then he enjoyed it.

My interest in J.B.'s ethics may too much enchant me. They may even paralyze my service to him. They have an old proverb here on Muddyscuttle. "Fools rush in where angels fear to tread." It is somewhat comforting to know that here at least they separate fools and angels. I must be careful that I do not bring the categories closer.

When moral love flows broad as seas
Men too grow moral: straight as trees.

Alleluia,
Valiant

Snow

I AM REELING AT THE CIRCUMSTANCES. The first snow of winter has left everything whiter than it was. Glory has fallen with the snow. During a long and gentle snowfall, J.B. met Cassie at Henry VIII. While this may sound like a historical museum, it is but a bar. I noticed that Alphalite was in a supreme state of elation. He was buzzing in and out of walls and making frequent Alleluias. It is good that we sing in other dimensions or the bar would have exploded with the volume of his joy.

The fireworks—if the Committee will permit such a terrestrial cliche—began when J.B. offered to buy Cassie a highball and she declined. J.B. had his "usuals," which is no longer unusual, since he is having them unusually often. Cassie clearly had something on her mind that she knew J.B. would find unpleasant. J.B. insisted that she loosen up with him by having one of her usuals. "J.B.," she said, "I don't want to loosen up. I know what happens every time we get 'loose.'"

J.B. was afraid. "Come on, Cassie, let's unwind—I've got a new kind of chablis I want you to try when we get to my place. It's going to be a great evening!"

"Not for me!" said Cassie.

Cassie was afraid that for her refusal, J.B. would call her a "prude" right on the spot. A prude in Muddyscuttle usage is an over-virtuous woman. There is such colloquial malice in the word that American women would rather do anything than be labeled by such a term. There are whole movements of women in this hemisphere that have dedicated themselves to the extinction of such labels.

J.B. looked into his drink, studied the ice cubes, and then blurted out, "What are you, Cassie, some kind of prude? For God's sake!"

"Yes, it is rather for his sake, I suppose," she said.

"Whose sake?" thundered J.B., banging his glass of ice cubes on the small table.

"God's."

"God's? Don't tell me you're getting mixed up with God. You're not only a prude, but a God-nut. . . . Cassie, for Christ's sake!"

"His, too!" she said in the face of his hard anger.

A long period of silence followed. It seemed for a moment she might abandon her prudery and agree to go home with him. I have not seen two souls more in agony than they appeared to be. I could tell she wanted to please J.B., but even more than that, she seemed possessed of a new allegiance. He could neither understand nor accept it. She wanted to have a little drink with him, but was afraid that even one might weaken her resolve. He stared at the bottom of his glass.

After an agonizing silence, she spoke nervously, but she was firm.

"Look, J.B., let's face it. We have a cheap relationship, always plastered over with too much booze and a lot of cheap scenes in your apartment."

Alphalite beamed.

"It never bothered you before," he said.

"Well, it does now, since . . ."

"Since what?" he almost shouted. He was talking so loudly that several others in the bar turned their heads and stared in the direction of their table.

"Since what?" he asked again, not quite so loudly.

"Well," she hesitated. The words were coming hard for her.

"Since what . . . since what . . . SINCE WHAT?"

"Since I accepted Christ."

Alphalite began buzzing excitedly through the walls again. J.B. blurted out a coarse laugh and slapped his leg in cruel

attack. "You accepted Christ! . . . How could you do that?"

I felt sorry that J.B. was so acid to Cassie. The idea of Cassie "accepting Christ" bothered me some, too. The idea is so humanized somehow. Who are these mortals that they condescend to accept or reject the Logos? The key issue never seems to surface in their small system of arrogance. "Accept Christ" is the way that some Scuttlers in the evangelical world refer to reclamation. I know you will be galled by reading this, for it seems they may have missed the point. Their way of putting it leaves the Almighty under human judgment. Salvation is born in Christ's condescending to accept man, and not man stooping to accept the unworthy love of God. It makes a wreck of excellence.

We dare not dwell long on this kind of human arrogance. The way they speak of it, Christ is life, offered to them on a silver platter, and they ponder whether they will condescend to accept his magnificent sacrifice. What's for them to accept? They should beg his favor. If they miss it, indeed, all that is left to them is Daystar's pit. How fashionable of them to make their rescue from the pit sound like some sort of bargain for God! What drowning man confers laurels upon the lifeguard because he has been so lucky as to rescue his resplendent victim?

Since so many speak of it this way, we must not be too hard on Cassie for so phrasing it. In the course of this tense conversation, Cassie told J.B. that she had been visited by two visitors from Grace Church who had told her about Christ. "Suddenly," she said, "I realized how far I was from the path. I confessed my sin, and I plan to go to church on Sunday. I was hoping you might come too, J.B."

"You're talking like my funny aunt," he replied.

"Ida?" asked Cassie.

J.B. nodded.

"But you always told me you loved your aunt as anyone else would have loved their mother."

"She's been a mother to me, but she's a God-nut just like you,

Cassie," he fumed. He seemed suddenly ashamed that he had referred to Aunt Ida with such despicable terms. "Look, Cassie," he said, tempering his volume with calm, "if not tonight, couldn't we get together at my apartment this weekend and talk the whole thing over?"

"Not anymore. . . . I'm sorry, J.B. Not this weekend or any weekend. Not tonight or any night! I've come across a new set of standards. I shall need Christ's help to live up to them."

He was offended by the way she spoke of "Christ's help." It is quite out of fashion on Muddyscuttle to just blurt out the words "Jesus" or "Christ," unless one is using them in a coarse context. To use the words in the open as you might use the name of William or Eric is socially taboo.

Soon conversation turned from Cassie's new experience to Grace Church. "What's this place like if it sends out God freaks to menace decent American neighborhoods?" asked J.B.

"What's so decent about my neighborhood?" She answered his question with one of her own.

"Well . . . it's . . . "

"I'll tell you what kind of people live in my neighborhood. They drink too much, make free sex their lifestyle, and are starved to death for any real piers upon which to build their lives."

"You sound like Frankie Williams."

"Maybe our neighborhoods need to be menaced. Maybe the entire nation could use what I have found. Maybe you need it, J.B. What if your Aunt Ida is right?"

"I still can't fathom people talking about God right in the streets, or in their homes, or in lounges like this, for Christ's sake!"

"That's exactly . . . "

"I know, I know, I know—that's exactly whose sake it's for."

"And the people who speak openly of Christ are not weird. They seem to me to be the only ones in touch with their world. One of the men who shared the Christ-life with me works for your company. His name is Beau Ridley."

"Beau Ridley! I know him. He seemed so intelligent, too. He's the guy who says prayer in the company cafeteria before he eats . . . I'll be damned!"

"Could be, J.B."

"Cassie, will you quit interrupting me with these innuendos! . . . Beau Ridley," he said, collecting himself. "The man's a fanatic! Maybe even a lunatic! So he was one of the—how do you say it?—witnesses who came to your door."

"Yes."

"That phony. How can you let a religious nut like that ruin our great relationship?"

"It wasn't a great relationship. It was cheap! I want out, J.B."

J.B. grew red with anger. "You were never in, Baby!" he yelled at her.

She picked up her coat and purse and walked out into the snow. Alphalite appeared for a moment in the open doorway, and I could see the snow falling.

Alphalite called back in language beyond them, but expressed the wisdom of new creation. "White is a majestic color, Val."

"Indeed!" I called back.

Only blackness ever knows
The shining treasure of the snows.

Alleluia,
Valiant

The Fire and Image

WE ARE ALONE TONIGHT. J.B. has had several more of his usuals and isn't thinking very clearly. There is a fire in his fireplace. The room is hot and, yet, there is a chill about it all. He is sweltering from an odd fever set into his system by two loves. One love is the attachment he feels to Cassie, which I thought was only a sexual convenience. Tonight it is becoming clear that she means more to him than I had before supposed.

The second love is the new love he observed in Cassie. He is almost jealous of her new love for Christ. How can one really be jealous of such an exalted and different kind of love? Yet, he is. Besides this jealousy, he is seething in resentment that Christ has apparently doomed him to lonely weekends.

While he was staring at the fire, the dancing flames seemed to hold him mesmerized. "Why . . . why . . . did she do it? . . . I need her so . . ." he muttered, looking again into the fire. "Oh, hell!" he said, throwing his glass against the mantle. It shattered and fell upon the hearth. He barely had spoken the words when the imagery of his words fell upon the flames.

He remembered the fire! It was hell! That fire so long ago had left him an orphan. He remembered how lonely he felt when he knew his parents were still in their incendiary tomb that had been his tight little world. The teddy bear that had been his only surviving toy still glared at him from its slouched position on the corner of the bureau near the window. "Hell!" he said again.

The fire flickered.

Images of things long gone danced in the bright embers.

He beheld himself as a boy wandering on the lawn among the great hoses and red lights. He remembered the fire and his immense gratitude that Aunt Ida had come. How he had clung to her in the most welcome embrace of his life! She had been so different from his own parents. Her love, while only a kind of substitute for the new loneliness that was his, seemed rooted in the firm soil of Kentucky. How he needed the depth of compassion that lived in that good country woman!

Now he wondered if Aunt Ida would even recognize him. He was drunk, lonely, and maudlin over his old rag toy. Nor would International Investors have recognized this budding young executive, oiled in martinis, crying over his teddy bear, and cowering before the spectres that rose from his fireplace to walk his troubled thoughts.

He got himself a drink. With bleary eyes he walked over to the little bear and picked it up. He smiled and felt the pain of bittersweet memories. He set the bear down, and by odd coincidence, its soft left leg fell upon the Bible. He picked up the book. He stood with the amber flickering of the fireplace upon his young yet aging face. "What would Auntie think? My standing here with a Bible in one hand and a martini in the other?" he asked himself.

He thought of trying again to read it, but only thumbed its pages and set it down again. "Despair for nothing!" he said to himself. "I have it all: a fine job, a sports car, a good salary, and an apartment with the right address." Then Cassie's definition of her neighborhood rang again in the air about him: "I'll tell you what kind of people live in my neighborhood. They drink too much, make free sex their lifestyle, and are starved to death for any real piers upon which to build their lives." J.B. knew that this was not only her neighborhood, but his as well. Even more than his neighborhood, it was himself.

He looked above the glass. The former glass lay shattered on the hearth. The flame reflecting from the broken pieces seemed somehow to symbolize his life.

Then I urged J.B. to a new plateau. He has somewhat of a

strong mind, so I was able to manage this only because he was drunk and offered little resistance. I caused a vision to form on the amber tips of the flames that settled low above the glowing coals.

In the dying fire I managed to float the image of his old aunt as she had been years before. Among the smaller embers J.B. saw the adolescent image of himself. The dream lived. J.B. grasped his aunt. They embraced, and as the boy held her, she grew old and wrinkled, then faded and was gone.

He was alone. He knew he was.

Then there arose a teddy bear. It seemed friendly to him for an instant. Then it began to enlarge. Its scruffy little face changed as it grew. At last it towered above him in the room. It was fanged. His teddy—once his great security symbol—now menaced him. It beckoned him into the flames. He was afraid to follow. The hypnotic effect of the glowing coals fixed his trance. With effort at last he managed to close his eyes against the demon bear.

He turned himself from the fire and faced the icy windows. "Oh, Auntie, save me!" he said. The cold air near the frosted window brought him a new view of his world. He was ashamed he had cried out into the room. He turned and looked again and the demon was gone. The only bear in the room still stared at him from the bureau top.

"Well, I'll be damned," he said, but wished he hadn't.

The things that thump in semi-light
Can make men fear the pending night
That Heaven never sees.

Alleluia,
Valiant

Of Love
and
Backslipping

WHILE J.B. HAS NOT SEEN CASSIE since the big snow, I have learned something of her from Ridley's angel, Joymore. Cassie has learned that free love is costly in terms of guilt and self-acceptance. Her former weekends will not set free her present ones. Why did she ever live with J.B.?

Like other mortals, Cassie spends her time trying to understand herself. There are as many theories of human behavior as there are psychiatrists. Cassie has read many in her search for herself. There are moments of loneliness when she is tempted to call J.B. and opt for a return to her old lifestyle.

Evangelical churchmen on the planet talk of a problem that believers call backslipping. Backslipping is the human tendency to abandon the Logos-life and reenter a former value system. Most new believers return to old lifestyles when they begin to feel that they can handle life on their own without the necessity of faith. Backslipping usually begins in such self-sufficiency. Christ never taught self-reliance. He taught that he himself is the only source of confident living. Self-sufficiency is based upon a defective psychology which teaches that humans can do anything they think they can. Oh, that Cassie might learn quickly that there is a great chasm between her intention and ability!

I have heard that this strange idea of self-reliance begins in youth. Parents on Muddyscuttle allegedly tell their children about a little locomotive who was asked to pull a long line of cars up a hill. The "choo-choo" is a positive thinker who manages to succeed because he believes so much in himself. He goes along the rails saying, "I think I can, I think I can." Humans often read this tale to their children as an early parable of self-sufficiency. The story is probably a part of Cassie's distant past.

Alphalite told Joymore that Cassie sees herself as omni-capable. Her petty arrogance dismisses most of her need for our Beloved Logos. Her tyranny lies in making God her partner in a faith venture. Like most other positive-thinking Christians, she has two sides: hers and the one which is not so crucial. She has mistakenly felt that the Logos is on her side and is assisting her in a kind of spiritual imperialism to "rise to the top of life." She believes that faith in the Logos gives her the right to control others and be successful, whatever devious path she follows.

She has already read some of the numerous books and magazines on the subject. She has, therefore, heard a score of Christians testify how God exists for our own personal advancement in life. "How to Be Successful" reads one such article. "Jesus Made Me Corporate Head" reads another. "Christ Gave Me the Winner's Cup in Swimsuit Competition" reads another. From what Alphalite tells me, she is still unable to see that her idealism is naive and motto-ridden. She, like many new believers, reads bumper stickers more than the Bible. There are any number of popular cliches on self-sufficiency. "Turn Your Aches to Steaks" says one; another reads, "Jesus Don't Sponsor No Flops." These are simple slogans of self-sufficiency which, attached to human efforts, displaces the need of Christ.

My fear is that Cassie may be diverted into egocentric Christianity and become unconcerned about J.B.'s need for Christ. That must not happen; her own new faith is the most immediate hope my client has of being reclaimed. Should she backslip at this point, my ardent hope for J.B. would suffer. He is clearly "in love with her" and so smitten by this romantic madness that he would be most open to anything Cassie said. Oh, that she knew this!

Even though I know my time here is short, I must remind the Committee that I am struggling on through storms of homesickness. I have caught myself distracted at cocktail parties as J.B. has his usuals. I feel a certain planetary revulsion in these moments. I find myself singing the silent songs of infinity. How long a human year can seem when one is separated from the Logos! J.B.'s Cassie does not really want to go to Heaven now: she is snared in the sociology of earthly life and, like other Muddyscuttlers, doesn't want to die at all. Earth, not Heaven, is the residence she most desires.

All Christians sing of the glory of going to Heaven, but no one wants to be on the next load. Leaving the planet is for them a gruesome disinheritance. It is because they love too low. Heaven for them is a great privation where they cannot glut on all their various appetites. Heaven is a dull place without shopping malls, football, television, and ice cream. Heaven is just a better hell, really, than the one with flames and demons; but can heaven be heaven with neither sex nor martinis? Heaven is just below whatever they happen to enjoy. Deep in their hearts they would rather keep all the goodies of their current lives and build such heavens as they can. Even seeing Christ is scarcely prize enough to replace the disinheritance that death will bring them.

They are all afraid of death, and this fear is so natural to them that even the love of Logos does not set them entirely free. With some Christians it is not so much death they fear, but the dying. Dying is not just losing Muddyscuttle, but the pain that comes in the process of losing it.

Oh, how I long for the world that neither J.B. nor Cassie can ever imagine while they are prisoners in protoplasm! Always they indulge their flesh and starve their spirits. I know I grumble far too much—I am, as I have said, most homesick. If only I could hear again a great celestial chorus.

At my last rehearsal, the Cogdillians were performing the anthem for Clockstop called "Valiant the Rider in Splendor and Power." It is a magnificent piece whose strains will not settle from my spirit. I remember that the bass accompaniment was an exploding supernova and a comet storm. I do so anticipate giving up these shallow orchestrations that Muddyscuttlers call music. It offends all taste. Has the Committee ever heard of a "jukebox?" The deepest part of Daystar's pit must be long arcades filled with these raucous devices.

J.B. loves these but still swelters in meaninglessness, precisely because he has no real way of perceiving our parallel universe. He suffers from nearsightedness, seeing nothing but the obvious, loving only the transient. He sings only jukebox music and, sadly, never suspects the gallant anthems of our realm.

Valiant the rider in splendor and power
Comes upon light and the thunder of force.
Eternity bridles the steed of the hour
And glory unfolds at the source of the source.

Alleluia,
Valiant

A Muddyscuttle Fear

I HAVE GREATLY DESIRED TO pass along some spiritual counsel to Alphalite. But I still have not seen him since that last exchange between J.B. and Cassie in the bar. It has not been long in our reckoning of time, but it has been two weeks for them. I do hope Cassie is still "sticking to her guns," as Muddyscuttlers often say of determined resolve.

One crucial event and several interesting ones have befallen J.B. First of all, J.B. took a business trip to a city called Los Angeles. I was hoping it really would be a city of angels, but to my dismay it held the same proportion of angels and guardians that exists elsewhere on the planet.

Most interesting to me was the flight itself. I have never enjoyed time on an airship. How cumbersome and slow the odd things go, and yet they call it flight. How pedestrian is human science! We were lumbering along at such a snail's pace, I wonder that we did not fall upon the planet. It would not have been a long fall, but you know how prone these humans are to injury and death. None would have survived.

Two things happened that caused J.B. to think later of both Christ and Cassie's changed values. The first occurred when the plane made an intermediate stop in a city called Denver. J.B. was approached in the air terminal by a strange group of young people wearing colored robes and chanting strange words I could not recognize. Neither did J.B. They approached him near a newsstand where he had planned to buy a magazine that he refers to as a "girlie book." I will not distract myself to explain "girlie" to the Committee.

He never bought the magazine because these strange young people were trying to sell him a holy book of their own. I reminded J.B. that he had not even read the Holy Bible that his Aunt Ida had given him. I warned him to be careful about buying books of which his Aunt Ida would not approve. The impact of my suggestion was strengthened by J.B.'s reflecting about Cassie and his Aunt Ida and their elusive similarity. He was smitten in conscience and bought neither the holy book nor the girlie magazine.

Later in his hotel room in Los Angeles, J.B. made a discovery as he was standing before the mirror shaving. He noticed a large swelling just under his jaw. He stroked it, felt it, and tried to make it retreat into his neck, but he could not. He seemed alarmed by its defiant appearance.

The next morning it was still there. He had a certain uneasiness each time he beheld it in the mirror. It caused him some pain, and he shaved that section of his neck more gently than the rest of his face. However, his concern did not slow his drinking. He has been hitting the bottle harder than ever these days. He seems to have lost interest in the fairer sex. His relationship with Cassie is "on the rocks." By odd coincidence, that is the way he drinks his Scotch—though I feel sure the metaphors are not connected.

He does confuse me with his feelings. He told one of the accountants in his carpool that he thought he might be "carrying a torch" for Cassie. One hopes he will "carry his torch" while she "sticks to her guns." (Aren't these cliches dreadful?) I shall need both his love of her and her commitment to Christ to draw him on toward reclamation.

We returned from Los Angeles on a non-stop flight. Human aviation would beggar a handicapped angel. They have two good wings on these contraptions, yet they dawdle along at the speed of sound. I could certainly have flown faster outside the plane.

It was most disconcerting to learn that J.B. could get his usuals even on the airplane. Of course, he did. He never passes them up. He is drinking out of a general lack of interest in life. He may have a touch of Muddyscuttle depression called the "blahs," which only makes his drinking worse.

I am sure now that he is in love. Can you help understand this condition of violent infatuation that these humans experience? I wish J.B. would see Cassie long enough for me to see Alphalite. I would like to find out how she has been behaving. She could possibly be "carrying a torch" as well as "sticking to her guns."

At work yesterday J.B. agreed to have lunch with Beau Ridley, Joymore's charge.

This could be a new breakthrough for the Logos. I am still doing my Alleluias with joy even when J.B. mopes about his apartment with the blahs. I dare not cease my Alleluias, lest I lose my joy. Think of me.

When any realm learns how to love
The universe rejoices.

Alleluia,
Valiant

A Special Word to the Committee

MY DAYS GROW SHORT, my conflicts violent. Here is the essence of my inner wrangling. Humans know only a lateral geography east and west and whatever the other two directions are. They know nothing about the upper and lower dimensions. This is most unfortunate because east is about like west, but upper is immensely better than lower, as I am now discovering. Christ is the example of obedience for both humans and angels. He left Upperton for Muddyscuttle because he loved the Lord High Command, who loves every living being in the universe.

I have often marveled at this creation when I can see no reason for its being. I have heard of the planet Hopeton that is similar to Muddyscuttle. It lies yet unspoiled in the starlets of Firehalls Down. It is a lovely stopover where men are as pure as angels, holding the exact same values. What a world it must be! Still, loving unlovely worlds is the best evidence that the High Command exists. I marvel how the Logos once wept over the lost humans of this planet. At the end of his humanization he grieved their estate even though their behavior was reprehensible. But when he opened his mouth, even dying as he was, he only begged God to forgive the cruel planet.

All Upperton fell and wept.

Now I am learning how much this fallen planet means to God. Take J.B., for instance. I too care for him. I maintain a secret hope for J.B.'s Aunt Ida. According to a friend of mine in Human Petitions, she is regular in her prayers and many of her petitions focus on her dear nephew. She is concerned for "his

soul," as she phrases it. So there are at least two of us down here who care. Perhaps Cassie is praying for J.B. too, but I cannot be sure.

The lump on J.B.'s neck may have little relevance, but it is getting larger, and he is frightened. My clients on earlier tours also became concerned about the various lumps and bumps that came on them from time to time. I do remember that some of the lumps were called "mumps." (You would think they would have called them lumps.) While they caused my charges a great deal of discomfort, I couldn't help thinking about how humorous they were, these "mumps." Oh, the great day when both J.B. and I will be free of mumps and bumps and time!

Mumps seem not to be so terminal a state as being "in love." It has such a profound effect on my client. He is lost these days, rubbing his poor neck and grieving Cassie's absence. He can barely stand to eat. Whether you on the Committee can accept it or not, J.B. is "in love." And shallow as it may seem in Heaven, it is a deep matter in Cleveland.

Small men and tiny worlds should know
Great love will make a planet grow.

Alleluia,
Valiant

January

HERE IS THE ASTOUNDING NEWS! J.B. went to a physician, who told him he must enter a hospital as soon as possible. The doctor said the unusual swelling could be lymphatic carcinoma. This is a serious human condition and far more dreaded than mumps. J.B. is to have a biopsy immediately.

He was so alarmed that he quickly called Aunt Ida and asked her to pray. Aunt Ida plans to come to Cleveland straightway. The biopsy may be immediately preliminary to more serious surgery.

J.B. is so frightened he is trying to read the Bible again. He threw away most of his girlie books, keeping only the best, which are really the worst. He has been trying to live in a way he feels will please his Aunt Ida. This is a secondary reason for being good, at least when compared with the higher motives of the saints. But while he is being good for all the wrong reasons, he is managing an unbelievable amount of reform. He is to go into the hospital next Monday.

Here is the spectacular news! He is going to church with Beau Ridley on Sunday. I think there are two reasons. First, he knows that Cassie attends Grace Church, and he is anxious to catch a glimpse of her. Second, he is frightened by the prospect of surgery. He hopes to make a last-minute impression on God. "I would like to get God on my side," he said, accepting Beau's invitation.

He and Beau had an interesting conversation over dinner. I must try to tell you exactly what transpired. They ordered a rather expensive human food called lobster tails. I wish I could draw you a picture of these delicacies as they lay on the plate. When I saw these tails, I wondered what their heads must have looked like. Anyway, after the food was served, Beau asked if he could say grace.

"Grace? Right here in the restaurant?" asked J.B.

"Yes . . . if that's all right?" asked Beau.

"Why yes, I . . . I guess so."

Beau did pray rather loudly, and J.B. looked around at other guests and smiled nervously. Mercifully for J.B., Beau's prayer was short.

"I used to pray when I was a boy," said J.B. sheepishly.

"Oh, really. . . . Do you now?" Beau responded.

"Not so much. . . . In fact, I leave that to my Aunt Ida. She's more regular than a preacher."

"What did you pray when you were a boy?"

"Oh, you know. . . . Now I lay me down to sleep, I pray the Lord my soul to keep. If I should die . . ." At this point, J.B. stopped and felt his neck lump. He seemed choked for a moment and then continued, ". . . before I wake, I pray the Lord my soul to take."

Taking a bite of his lobster tail, Beau asked, "And if you did, would he?"

"If I did would he do *what?*" J.B. responded, making it clear Beau's question was confusing.

"If you should die before you wake . . . would he take your soul?" asked Beau.

"I . . . I . . . I guess so. I mean, my Aunt Ida is a special friend of his and . . . I . . . "

"I'm sure she is, but Christ will not accept you on the basis of family faith. Your Aunt Ida's faith cannot avail for you. J.B., you need a relationship of your own with Christ, just like your friend Cassie has."

By this time J.B. was ill at ease. He clawed at his collar, then seized on Cassie's name, "Have you seen Cassie lately?"

"Yes. She has become regular at church. I frequently see her in worship. Cassie seems to have made a sincere commitment to Christ . . . but she seems a little lonely. . . . My wife seems to think she's in love . . ."

"With whom? How can your wife tell?" J.B. seemed to be on the edge of apoplexy.

"She may be entirely wrong," said Beau. "Women seem to understand these things. I'm quite pleased with Cassie's determination to serve Christ. She really seems to be 'sticking to her guns.' You know, I think my wife may be right. She does seem a little misty-eyed and faraway. I think she may be 'carrying a torch' for someone."

I was delighted with Ridley's insight. So, she is "carrying a torch" and "sticking to her guns" after all. It was welcome news.

The conversation resulted in J.B.'s promising to attend Grace Church Sunday morning. In the afternoon he'll be going to the hospital shortly after Aunt Ida arrives in Cleveland, so his Sunday will be busy.

There is one more aspect of glory. Frankie Williams is coming to Municipal Arena with his Greater Cleveland Conquest. Beau mentioned it to J.B. He said he would be counseling inquirers on the floor each evening.

Maybe all these circumstances will leave my client open to a new consideration of the Logos. J.B. seems to be more spiritually sensitive in every area. I don't mean to bore the Committee with trivia, but J.B. actually tipped his hat to a nun. Perhaps it is not a great sign in itself, except that in heart J.B. was thinking, "I must see what these creatures believe that gives them the ability to live without sex." Celibacy to J.B. is an insane idea. Still, he sees it as a great achievement for those with the affliction.

I am hopeful that with the lump, Aunt Ida, Frankie Williams, Beau Ridley, Grace Church, and above all, Cassie, maybe J.B. will soon discover the Logos. Ah, if it happens! Greatness will come! J.B. will see a world where he can be of service. He will hear the cry of orphans for the first time. He will see the dispossessed and homeless. He will read beyond his questionable magazines the literature of a suffering world. He will be born anew to the possibilities of a life that is courageous enough to look upon all the hurt that exists just beyond the blind indulgence of all his cravings.

Come, Logos!

A star exploded and
The fiery band
Held at its heart
The Great Command: Go! LOVE!

Alleluia,
Valiant

Star
Thoughts

THINGS SEEM TO BE COMING my way at last. I must "strike while the iron is hot," as they say in Cleveland. My fear is that I may be pinning too many of my hopes upon the coming Frankie Williams Conquest.

The danger of conquests is that they are often emotional in their appeal. Conversion at its basic level is the sovereignty of the Logos. Only last week I learned that several were turned back at the gates of Upperton. They had terminated in a car crash on the way home from some evangelistic worship services. They had arrived at the gates singing sweetly a song they had heard at the conquest. It was with some terror that they were turned back, for they had no real knowledge of Christ.

I am always sad for those who have a form of religion but fail to understand real faith. No one is admitted to Upperton except those filled with the substance of the Logos. I cannot allow my client to rely on shallow understanding. The world swelters under a thousand griefs: death, war, hate. He must be reclaimed or he will never care about the things Upperton cares about.

During the humanization of Christ, he observed much shallowness of spirit. He warned all Muddyscuttlers, "Not everyone who cries Logos shall enter Upperton, but he who does the will of the Lord High Command." It is the will of the Lord High Command for men to fill their hollow existence with service to a broken world.

My client must constantly face this issue of inwardness. Upperton is off-limits to Scuttlers whose only attribute is outwardness. I remember a surprised atheist who came to the gates unable to believe he was still alive when he knew he wasn't. He was trying to get into Heaven without that inwardness that is the one inviolable standard of Upperton. He was honest, having come straight from the philosophy department of a large university. He kept mumbling that he had many degrees and had never seriously believed in either Heaven or God. He assured us that he finally knew that both were as real as his doctor of philosophy degree. But he was so late in coming to us that, of course, we could do nothing to help.

I fear that J.B. may be frightened into shallow commitment by this lump. He may make some spurious decision to regain Cassie's lost esteem. I must hurry him to better understanding. He must receive Christ out of his own sense of spiritual desperation or he, too, will be turned from the gates.

Most Scuttlers have fuzzy notions about what it takes to be admitted. I once knew a man who arrived at the gates of Heaven offering the God-and-Nationhood badge he once earned in Young Campers. He insisted it wasn't fair to turn him out of Heaven when he had helped so many little old ladies across the street. I would have helped if I could, but the imperative inwardness was missing, so I was powerless.

J.B. must come to understand that the nature of conversion lies in Christ's demand that true penance be offered in place of human arrogance, or inwardness has no validity.

Christians have a way of codifying and reducing the mysteries of their spirituality to cliches. (This grievous tendency is behind the "Honk-If-You-Love-Jesus" syndrome.) One American evangelist from the Bible Belt codified the mystery of salvation in a most curious metaphor. He called it the "Thessalonian Turnpike to Salvation." There were three lanes on the Thessalonian Turnpike, he said: Lane One, all must turn from sin to be saved; Lane Two, all should follow

Jesus to be saved; Lane Three, we must turn to the living God to find salvation. His approach was little different from one of J.B.'s sales seminars. Here's how one uses the Thessalonian Turnpike: First, one rings the doorbell (while the angels presumably come to attention) and says, "Excuse me, sir, but if Jesus were to come this minute, would you be holding a harp or a pitchfork?" If the answer is "harp," fine, but if "pitchfork," then you should begin the presentation of the "Thessalonian Turnpike to Salvation."

My fear is that J.B. could be led down the path of Christianity where the machinery is great and the mystery is small. Although I will rejoice at any experience which brings him to Christ, he must know that salvation is in the Logos alone and not the rote schemes that evangelicals use to pry the gates of Heaven open. Muddyscuttlers ever obscure the Great Chair with petty formulas.

Once more my hope rides on circumstance. I must trust in the combined influences of Aunt Ida, the neck lump, Frankie Williams, Grace Church, and Beau Ridley . . . and, of course, Cassie.

Praise all human need and place
Where the wounded hand of joy
Beckons littleness to Grace!

Alleluia,
Valiant

The Rural Saint

I AM IN CHURCH TRYING to focus on the sermon. This pastor *can* communicate. His sermon is on life after death. Nothing could be better for J.B. His neck lump being what it is, he is most concerned about his future and is trying to get all the information on Heaven he can. So J.B. is listening hard.

This sermon on Heaven is obviously being preached by a man who has never been there. Yet those here this morning are listening intently as though he has just come back from the place. Fortunately, they are unable to see the pastor's guardian, who is standing right beside him grimacing at the parson's naivete. How shall humans ever learn what angels find so commonplace?

Perhaps the Committee can tell by my last entries that, while my enthusiasm is better, I am still suffering from the dingy illumination of Muddyscuttle. At least this sermon makes me see again the delightful world that is only a few months away now. I anticipate the glorious day I shall return to Upperton. I shall blink for days in the incandescence.

I am glad J.B. is at least hearing of the other world this morning. How he needs to learn of it! He will never be allowed in Heaven because he tips his hat to female clerics. I must say, it is deflating to leave my own celestial preoccupation and deal with nuns and bumper stickers. But I am trying to keep our friendship usable across the reaches of our very different worlds. And sermons like this one do bring our worlds closer. J.B. doesn't know it, but only as he accepts my world will his really have any meaning.

I have continued to meditate upon the words of the pastor. Perhaps that is the mark of a great sermon. It was clear even as he spoke that he had never been to Upperton, and yet there was a fundamental worth to all he said. It was he himself that impressed me. What the man was preceded all he said; isn't it always that way?

He was in league with the angels. He was standing firmly on the planet but free of materiality. He spoke about the reality of the Logos and cried in an honest passion I have not seen to date on this orb. Mystery clung about him, and yet, he was stripped to a nudity of soul and power of essence. He seemed to give full human vision to those things which do not appear. His manhood was there, but only the slightest encumbrance to his inwardness. His words, gilded with joy, flew at J.B.'s encrusted resistance.

J.B. had attended these services to see Cassie. She sat a half-congregation away from him, but once the sermon began, he never saw her again. He did see his sodden interior and his thin veneer of respectability. He was close to reclamation as the sermon ended—I am sure of it.

After the service Cassie greeted him with reservation, but welcomed him to the services of *her* church. (Evangelicals tend to be possessive of churches. They know the church belongs to the Logos, but you rarely hear them say so.) J.B. *is* in love. He was dying for her to say something, anything, to him. She maintained her reserve. He asked if he might call her sometime, but she said that there was too much between them. She told him she needed to put some distance between her past and herself. "I would prefer that you not call," she said kindly but firmly.

She turned to walk away when he said, "Very well, Cassie . . . if you would remember to say a little prayer for me, I'd appreciate it. I am going into the hospital today. My doctor is concerned that I may have a malignancy. I'm distressed . . . frightened, I guess."

Cassie turned back and tried to speak. She choked. She tried a second time, but was still overcome with emotion. Finally, saying nothing, she turned and walked away. Her steps were weighted with an agony of soul that made it clear even to J.B. that she was in love. In spite of the agony of this abruptness, he was ecstatic to see her so visibly affected.

Alphalite told me in a brief exchange that Cassie has been picking at her food and is very much in love. He says she is determined not to tell J.B. because of her love for the Logos. She still feels a lot of guilt over her past relationship with my client. She will not leave her past where she lived it. She presumes against our Logos by not letting him forgive the kind of life that she and J.B. once shared.

Cassie's friends at Grace Church have counseled her to forgive herself all that she has already been forgiven by the Logos. She should live in the freedom of reclamation. Still, she suffers. To be guilty of guilt is a great affront to God. Guilt is man's great reprimand. Muddyscuttlers are so reluctant to let our Logos provide atonement; there is ever the feeling that they must pay for their own sins. As if they could! Why can't they accept the overcoming power of crucifixion they forced upon the Beloved? What is this foolish notion that they can pay for their sins just by feeling bad about them after they have been fully forgiven in Heaven? How dare they think their little acts of self-incrimination are even visible beside the grandeur of his sacrifice? Yet that's what homemade atonement is: The foolish attempt to purchase forgiveness with guilt.

J.B. ate a lonely lunch after the services. He drove to the airport to pick up Aunt Ida, who arrived on one of those dawdling airships I mentioned earlier. She got off the plane with a small valise and a large Bible. J.B. was most happy to see her! I spent a few moments getting reacquainted with Nova, Ida's angel. He's a regular sort, solidly attendant. Nova says that, while Ida has certain idiosyncrasies I might find tedious, she practices utter submission to Christ.

After the initial hug and kisses, J.B. and Ida passed some idle chatter. He said he had been living just "like she had taught him." He was uncomfortable with his own words. She promised to make him kolaches and liver dumplings just as soon as he was out of the hospital. (Aunt Ida was once married to a Slavic man who ate unusual food.) This promise did not seem an incentive to health to me, but it did to him. I suppose it was not too unusual for someone who eats lobster tails.

After visiting for an hour or so about old acquaintances and their welfare, Ida drove J.B. to the hospital. He checked in and went to his room. As soon as he was dressed in curious bedclothes, Aunt Ida came in and visited until his supper was served. At one point the dialogue became interesting. Nova and I made some rough notes on what they were saying, and here is how it went:

Aunt Ida asked him with great concern, "Jay-Jay, are you worried about your surgery?"

J.B. answered with more than a little anxiety, "What will I do, Auntie, if it is cancer?"

"Do you remember what I taught you when Uncle Harvey was alive?"

"You taught me so many things, Auntie, I can't think of which one you mean right now."

Aunt Ida became forceful. She leaned on the hospital bed and moved in close and said, "Jay-Jay, I mean what I taught you about Jesus bein' the answer to your every problem. Are you still talkin' to Jesus, Jay-Jay?"

J.B. was clearly nervous. "Some, Auntie."

"Some! SOME! What are you saying?" Ida's voice rose higher. "I find that when people only say they are talkin' *some* to Jesus, they really aren't saying anything."

J.B. decided he would be honest. "Oh, Auntie, I can't lie to you. I don't talk to God. I didn't even think there was a God until recently ... now, I don't know. Maybe there is and maybe there isn't."

"Jay-Jay! What do you mean, you don't know if there is a God?" She became animated and wagged her index finger just under his nose. "Why, if Uncle Harvey—God rest his soul—could hear you talkin' this way, he'd turn you 'cross his overalls and give you what-for. He'd beat these funny notions out of your head for sure."

"I don't know if you can beat atheism out of people or pound God into them," he said.

"Maybe not, but it just isn't right for you to be here, created by the good Lord, and say the good Lord didn't make you. 'Member them little brown coveralls I made you in the third grade?"

"Uh-huh."

"Well, the coveralls had a maker, didn't they? And no matter how much you or anybody else would say they didn't they did." Ida's homespun logic seemed to J.B. like something he once dredged from a philosophy course—only more rustic.

"I know that, Auntie."

"Well, you're a lot more certain about the coveralls than you are about yourself, Jay-Jay. You think you just sorta sauntered into being without any God at all?"

"I dunno. Maybe."

"Maybe! Is that what your professors taught you down at that fancy school? When I think of all the money Uncle Harvey and I spent educating you, too. Did they teach you that there is no God? Did they teach you that he didn't make you whole and perfect?"

At this point she seemed to be through making her point. Then she gathered herself and began again without giving J.B. a chance to reply.

"Well, let me tell you, Jay-Jay, God made everything, and he made it whole and perfect. He never made anything that wasn't perfect and fine ... except, maybe atheistic college professors."

"And carcinoma, maybe. Did God make that, too, Auntie?"

"Aha! So that's it, isn't it, Jay-Jay! You're not so much doubting God as you're just plain mad at him! Well, why didn't you say that in the first place? Everybody gets mad at God every once in a while—even your Uncle Harvey!"

"Well, what's he ever done for me?" J.B. asked, waiting for Aunt Ida's wisdom to deposit some security on the threshold of his mind.

"What's he ever done for you?—I'll tell you what! He gave you an aunt and an uncle to care for you after your folks were killed in the fire. And he gave you a good mind and a college education. He gave you a good job. He gives you fifteen breaths a minute and a pulse of sixty-eight. He gave you . . . "

"Carcinoma!"

"No! A THOUSAND TIMES NO! He doesn't do things like that, Jay-Jay! But after everything else he's done for you . . . how can ya turn thumbs down on God? One little neck lump and you're all through with him, is that it?"

"Lately, Auntie, you'll have to admit, God's been walking by me and kicking me every chance he gets. I've got a better-than-average chance of cancer, and I've lost Cassie—"

"Cassie? Who's she?"

"Oh, nobody . . . just a girl I lived with . . . I mean . . . dated for a while, that's all."

"How'd you lose her?" asked Ida, probing uncomfortably as I cheered and winked at Nova.

"Well, she got religion and won't have anything to do with me anymore."

"Why not? What've you been up to that turns off decent folks?" Ida still probed.

"Er, nothing, Auntie. I'm decent . . . it's just that . . . ."

"Now, Jay-Jay, you gonna hold out on Auntie? What have you been doin' that isn't proper? You haven't been philandering 'round here in Cleveland, have you?"

"I don't want to talk about it anymore, Auntie. I have to be up early in the morning for the biopsy."

J.B. was perspiring by this time as Aunt Ida was clearly closing in. As she drew the strings of her pursuit, he became anxious. She opened her big black Bible and read him the most ominous words. "The fool hath said in his heart there is no God." Then she closed the book and took his hand and prayed with sincerity and great volume. She sounded like a prophetess in a thunderstorm.

"Now, God, Jay-Jay doesn't know any better than to say you don't exist. So you gotta help him, 'cause he's scared to death. God, if you wanna heal that little old lump on the side of his neck, you just take it away. I'm gonna have to ask you for this and trust you for it, 'cause poor Jay-Jay's in no shape to ask you for anything . . ."

Her tone became earnest, and tears began to flow from her tightly closed eyes. She continued:

"Oh, God, my poor Jay-Jay's been so lost in his sin and now Cassie's turned her back on him and his low ways. I pray you'll help him be more what he needs to be, not jus' so Cassie can respect him, but so he can respect himself. Mostly, God, give some direct attention to that little lump o' cancer under his jaw. I'm just trusting him to you and Jesus. Amen."

When Aunt Ida finished, she kissed him on the forehead. Shortly she gathered up her Bible and her handbag and left the hospital room. She had a less scholarly but deeper impact upon him than the pastor at Grace Church. He was glad to be alone and yet he wasn't. Nova and I could hardly take notes on their conversation for cheering Aunt Ida. She was magnificent! I hope we can get her into Upperton without revision.

Now the hospital is quiet. J.B. is not quite asleep. He's wishing that he had stayed after worship this morning to talk to the pastor. He is neurotic on most issues of the spirit. One moment he is an atheist and the next a desperate seeker. Still, in his seeking moments, he will not yield to Christ. He does seem to feel the burden of his previous life with Cassie; at such moments he feels he has sinned against God. The next moment ... there is no God. Human nature is fickle beyond description.

I am on the side of Nova's charge. How can any Muddy-scuttler stand in the middle of our universe and judge the Great Chair to be nothing at all? Human arrogance reaches its apex in atheism. I found myself wishing that Aunt Ida could become a mandatory lecturer to every university philosophy department. Her wisdom is uncongested. How well she understands the intellectual tendencies of men! They force God to be nothing and by this devious process rise to the spot God occupied before they deposed him. They are to be pitied.

Aunt Ida has a formulated faith, to be sure. Her view of sin is as small as J.B.'s, for different reasons. J.B. has been blinded to the great injustices of this world by his hedonistic ego. Ida's view of evil has been rehearsed in an atmosphere where drinking and sex are the little sins so often denounced while the universe aches with genocide and poverty.

But she is alive to the hurt that afflicts her world and she does care. She has demonstrated a quality of compassion that can come only from Christ and the whole substance of inwardness which he imparts.

Tomorrow my client shall know whether his life is to be shortened by disease. It is a heavy night for me. I love him and wish he didn't have to suffer. But from moments like these, our Beloved often gains a foothold in the human heart.

Come watch our Beloved leave footprints in air,
Evermore reigning where flesh may not dare.

Alleluia,
Valiant

A Silent Winter's Night

I T IS A LONG WINTER'S NIGHT. J.B. is waiting in dreamless sleep for tomorrow's surgery. He is "mixed up." I should think there is little "up" about being "mixed." I should rather have the cliche be "mixed down," since there is nothing elevated or lofty in the kind of indecision that J.B. now deals with.

J.B. may be deliberately choosing indecision because it is a safer way. Procrastination always eliminates the immediate risk. "The safest of all courses is to doubt," one old mortal said. In the battle for truth, doubt sometimes peeps cautiously over the ramparts to watch in safety while those who have courage state their convictions.

I cannot force J.B. out of his mixed condition. Uncertainty about values results in confusion. My client is always asking about the value of Christ-life while he clings to the value of life as it is. He thinks of conversion as the restrictions of a God who enjoys breathing down the collar of all who want to have a good time. J.B. accepts the axioms of his peers: "God is a kill-joy." Part of J.B. wishes to be under a higher dominion. On the other hand, his ego rebels fiercely in favor of his spurious independence from all outside spiritual intervention. The reclaimed often talk glowingly about the "Lordship of Christ" while they live in the egoistic glory of their own lordship. Here is their neurosis. Shall they have a Lord or be a lord? It keeps many from salvation, and it keeps most of the saved from deeper joy. Few resolve it.

Mortals have a burden that we guardians never deal with—flesh! I know I have earlier in this report lamented its absence at moments when I would like to give my client a reassuring touch. But for all the good qualities of flesh, I have never been able to understand the control this infernal substance has over spirit. What is it? Protoplasm? Bones? Follicles? Sinews? Whatever it is collectively, it makes demand. It drives earthlings until they become gluttonous in their appetites and overfill their every desire. And ultimately flesh destroys life, for it gets worn and old and diseased.

J.B. is sick—his flesh betrays his well-being. He suffers the curse of the neck lump! There is a real chance he could die from this cancerous betrayal of his own flesh. He cannot imagine getting on without this 180 pounds of flesh and blood he believes to be himself. So he lacerates himself with the possibility of disease. Oh, that he could see the liberation of spirit! It would end his captivity!

> *There comes but one great liberty*
> *When morning wakes the world to see*
> *That living after life is free.*

Alleluia,
Valiant

The Middle
of the Year

DURING THE NIGHT J.B.'s neck lump deflated and disappeared. The surgeon made a "preliminary incision" but found nothing. J.B. had extensive testing here at Memorial Hospital, but nothing has confirmed his early fears. It appears J.B. has been "healed," as churchmen say.

He is ecstatic! He is giving credit to Aunt Ida and God—in that order, I'm afraid. Aunt Ida has now asked the Lord to give him spiritual health as well. I owe the order and correctness of these notes to Nova.

When J.B. emerged from surgery groggy with anesthetic, he said with murky cheer, "Hi, Aunt Ida."

" 'Ello, Jay-Jay," replied his aunt. "Did you see the Lord in any of those dreams?"

"No, I didn't see anybody," he said. Then coming to himself, he quickly asked, "Is my surgery over?"

"It's all over. And best of all, there isn't anything under that big bandage on your neck."

"What's that?" he responded as though he had not heard her properly.

"It's all over. There isn't any neck lump. There wasn't when you went into surgery. The doctor said he'd never had a case like this. The tumor just seemed to go away in the night."

"What are you saying, Auntie? They didn't take the tumor off my neck?" His question represented his incredulity.

"They didn't need to, Jay-Jay. There wasn't any tumor there."

"That's amazing!"

"The word is miraculous! Your doctor said he thought it was amazing, too. But I asked him what was so amazing about the Lord healing my little Jay-Jay."

"Auntie, you're a marvel!" he said as if he had just faced the Virgin of Lourdes.

"Jesus is the marvel!" said Aunt Ida, giving the credit where it was due. "I'm just glad to be his child and able to see him work his marvelous power in every life—especially yours, Jay-Jay. I'm gonna pray right now and thank Jesus for beatin' these fancy doctors to that neck lump." So saying, she clamped her eyelids together and began.

"Now Jesus, you took care of Jay-Jay and healed him completely. I'm just gonna pray now that you'll help him quit saying you don't exist. He doesn't really mean anything by it, Lord. You know he's always been a questioning child and he thinks he's being honest with himself. At least now he knows that you can deal with cancer, and he needs to see you heal his doubts and confusion, too. Now, Lord, about his low life: you've seen ever'thing he's done—and I'm sure he's had the angels blushing 'round the throne. Lord, I pray you'll help him give up all his sin and think like Uncle Harvey and I raised him to think. And Lord, help Cassie— whoever she is—not to be too highbrow and goody-goody to help Jay-Jay till he comes around. Thank you for every little blessing from your mighty hand. In Jesus' name, Amen."

Much has transpired in the past twenty-four hours. Aunt Ida left yesterday, but I wish she was still here. There is a kind of power in her rural faith one does not often see around Cleveland.

There is one other incident you should know about. Cassie brought Jay-Jay . . . rather, J.B. . . . a box of nougats. It was good to see Alphalite again.

Cassie was delighted to learn of the "miracle." She said, "God, indeed, was merciful." J.B. was excited that she had come to see him—was surprised and delighted. She could not stay long. J.B. asked if he could phone her when he left the hospital. She said it would be okay, but she was becoming more involved in church activities and was often not home in the evenings. She said that she was going with the gang to a "Christian Life Seminar" and would be involved for several weeks. When the seminar was over, she agreed that he might call. J.B. asked her for a "goodbye kiss." She declined. She said they both had their lives to live, and little good could come of opening old wounds.

As she spoke of "wounds," she glanced at the bandage on J.B.'s neck, then quickly looked away as though it hurt her personally. She then walked briskly out of the room. She is determined not to be in love with him, though her determination seems to be weakening.

Beau Ridley called. Because of the "miracle," he was able to secure two promises. First, J.B. promised to go to Grace Church again on Sunday. Second, he agreed to attend the Williams Conquest of greater Cleveland when it begins next month.

In spite of the miracle, J.B. was glum the rest of the evening. I find myself participating ever so slightly in his mood. I understand Cassie's effort to break with her old way of life, but I almost wish she wouldn't be such a "prude."

On the day of a great "miracle," I am less hopeful than I should have supposed. J.B.'s healing, which seemed so glorious in the morning, was an uninteresting event by evening. I cannot understand how the glory of his miracle has so soon faded and does not mark his experience more deeply. Immediately after his recovery J.B. fastened a great deal of theological importance to the whole thing. And for his sake, it may be well. Still, contemporary miracles are less basic to the nature of faith than generally supposed. On their own, such great signs do little real good in helping people come to faith or in confirming them in it. Believers need, rather, that process of inwardness which feeds daily on spiritual substance. Only then will they adore Christ more than his miracles.

Oh, that he might know the Scriptures. Scuttlers suppose that if they could only see something "un" or "super" natural, they would immediately come to faith. Now J.B. has arrived at point-blank truth. God has affirmed himself in personal power at the point of J.B.'s need. He has seen the magnificent evidence of the supernatural. Yet he doubts. The miracle meant more to Aunt Ida than to J.B. She didn't need the miracle to believe in God; she believed in God as much before it happened. J.B. still disbelieves in spite of it.

Faith neither begins nor grows by miracles. The Logos chose the route of humanization in the glorious process of Muddyscuttle's reclamation. But this miraculous experience has never been witnessed by human beings as a whole. "Eye knowledge" is important to mortals. They have a proverb here that says "Seeing is believing." What a curious dependency! The corollary proverb is damning: "Not seeing is doubting."

Isn't it odd that having seen the supernatural, J.B. so soon regards it as natural? Why won't he learn that believing comes first and seeing later? If he would believe, he would see all that now mystifies and perplexes him. He would join those liberated Scuttlers for whom miracles are evidence to the heart and not the eye.

My client would be reclaimed already if he could accept his own spirituality. His thinking is materialistic. If he were pulverized to fine ash and scattered on the planet, nothing would change. He would still be J.B., as real as I am, without the curse of his own flesh obscuring his true existence. This is a cosmic riddle! It is a materialistic joke! By the time Muddyscuttlers discover genuine existence, it is too late to see the fleeting nature of materiality they once thought was true reality.

How slow is flesh! Hordes of humans followed Moses through Muddyscuttle wastelands. Time and again God performed magnificent miracles for them. He split seas, gave water from stone, and fed them bread from the desert floor! Did they believe, having seen? Not for long. They died doubting in aching blindness.

The great miracle of Jesus' humanization should produce faith. He divided loaves, walked on water, and drew the dead from coffins and tombs. His reward for all this was not belief, but humiliation and execution. At his death we in Upperton did not cry over the mutilation of his flesh—we knew that for what it was. It was the insult to love that left his Father reaching in agony from the Crystal Chair.

Some Scuttlers used to debate the question: Do miracles create faith, or does faith create miracles? Their question is absurd. Miracles transcend science and reason in demon-strating the supernatural realm. The one great miracle is reclamation. Most are reclaimed before they gain any per-ception of our realm. They meet Christ before they ever learn the significance of miracles. I must not despair. J.B. will be better motivated toward reclamation by his own sense of need than by Aunt Ida's miracle (and that is still how he refers to the neck-lump miracle).

When I am discouraged, I think of this. During his humanization, our Lord said, "If I be lifted up, I will draw all men to myself." It is not by little miracles, great arguments, nor threatening circumstances that men come to life everlasting. Life is Christ alone, eternal in power, pervading the cosmos, yet living in men and women. The great miracle is this reduction: the great Christ spiritually camping in small spirits.

Yet the Logos is the Lodestone. He will draw. I feel that J.B. may already be caught in the magnetism of Christ's life. Let us wait and see if he may not soon experience the only great miracle there is—the transformation of pitiful mortality into eternal life.

In the meantime I must clear the debris from the rails. Assail the barriers. Desire. Wait.

Miracles are frequent
And all the blind can see
A simple splendor coming
In dull complexity.

Alleluia,
Valiant

The Month
of the Logos

I AM COMING TO UNDERSTAND that faith is a matter of hearing. Words have immense power over mortals since they form the fabric of all reason. Cleveland is under siege by a new and powerful word that Frankie Williams calls the Word of God. This Word is now the subject of the press, and all souls who dwell in these environs seem stirred to stop and listen to it.

The Frankie Williams Conquest is in full swing, and J.B. has gone for the past three nights. Beau Ridley has been taking him to the Conquest, and Joymore and myself have derived great pleasure from these experiences. You may think me plane bound, but these arena services seem to smack of Upperton. Each night thirty thousand Scuttlers sing and pray for the reclamation of Cleveland. Best of all, there are thirty thousand guardians present, too. It is the best angelic singing I have heard since I left Cogdill. They are a superb evidence of what Guardians can really do in the rarified spiritual atmosphere of a fallen world. I know I have often railed upon the quality of religious music, but I have made an interesting discovery: one reason why mortal hymns are so bad is that mortals sing them. The same melodies, harmonies, and words are really quite beautiful when properly sung by our own kind.

The Conquest Songster is a fine human singer as he leads his stadium congregation. His guardian, Constellation, has been leading us guardians in the better music. If these Scuttlers could hear us, they might have an immedite experience of grace. Some of their hymns have dreadful lyrics that speak of human depravity and destitution. They really do not apply to us angels, but we sing them anyway. Here is a good example of their not-so-angelic lyrics:

> Just as I am and waiting not
> To cleanse my soul of one dark blot,
> To thee whose blood can cleanse each spot,
> O Lamb of God, I come!

But to mortals with what Aunt Ida calls "low ways," such lyrics are not so outlandish as they seem. Such ideas definitely need consideration.

Frankie Williams is a good evangelist. His words sear the human conscience. More than five hundred Scuttlers were reclaimed as the choir sang about human sin and spots and blots. How wholesome for them to consider their estate before our Beloved! Few such moments of truth and light occur upon this dismal orb.

Cleveland is aglow with a strange light. The High Command must have been overjoyed to see five hundred reclaimed at a single service. I doubt whether Upperton can imagine anything like this stadium full of men and angels joined in song. It was so ecstatic that we sang our way out of the arena and into the parking lots in a baptism of light.

Fervent angelic singing rose from those guardians whose clients were reclaimed. I wanted so to join them, but J.B. would not go forward. He listened to Frankie Williams intently but refused to budge throughout the invitation.

At one point J.B. appeared almost repentant and seemed as moved as he was the night Aunt Ida left him alone in the hospital room. He had resolved not to go forward and so clung to the stadium seat before him. He gripped the iron rail until his knuckles whitened. If he had released it for only a moment, he might have come to faith.

He is struggling against the Logos, but he is losing. He is being propelled to faith by a motivation stronger than I alone could compel. He is caught in the magnetism of the Spirit.

Now, about his romance.

Today he finally called Cassie. She seemed pleasant, but declined his offer of a lift to the Conquest tonight. Because she declined, he has decided to stay home. I am disappointed in this decision. J.B. is so close, and I desperately hope that Clockstop will be stayed until he is safely reclaimed.

One important incident you must know about. Yesterday J.B. and I had lunch with Beau Ridley and Joymore. Beau talked to J.B. of the Christ-life. He used a tool that the Committee will deplore—the Thessalonian Turnpike. I hope you will not think ill of Beau, for he does it with his whole heart. While I don't like the concept in general, it had a powerful effect.

Beau's earnest entreaty came cloaked with cliches. While he lacked John MacDonald's self-righteousness, his witness sounded similar:

"J.B., tell me this. Have you come to the place in your spiritual life that you know for sure if you were to die right now, you would be holding a harp instead of a pitchfork?"

"Well, I suspect it would be the latter," answered J.B. "All I know is that since I have been attending the Frankie Williams Conquest, I have been confused."

"That is just my point, J.B. Why do you think God had you and me become friends?"

"Was it God who did that? I didn't know that! I thought it just sort of happened because we both work for the same company and eat in the same lounge."

"No, J.B.! I've never found things that happenstance. God has a definite plan for even those events that seem small and insignificant." Beau seemed to speak with the tone of a bishop. "Everything that happens to us, God engineers in such a way to get us out from under our circumstances and put us under the blood."

"Under the blood? What's an unpleasant idea," objected J.B. "Besides, how can God, who is busy doing all the things he has to get done, manage to care about International Investors, much less the man in Cubicle 32?"

"The gospel is the great plan of a holy God. He wants everyone to get to know Jesus Christ. J.B., have you ever considered receiving Jesus as your personal Savior and getting saved by the blood?" Beau spoke in churchese, but J.B. responded in good faith.

"Oh, Beau, I don't know that much about God. At Grace Church and at the Conquest I think about the idea, but it looks impossible for me. Faith is easier for people like you than it is for those like me."

"Nonsense, J.B.!" protested Beau. "All things are possible through prayer. God can do anything but fail. You should really go after Jesus, 'cause where you go hereafter depends on what you go after here." Again the cliches flew.

J.B. became painfully honest. "I don't think I could be a good Christian even if I tried. I could never be as dedicated as you are, Beau. I've seen the changes in Cassie. I don't think I have the stuff it takes. Even if I could really make up my mind about God, I just don't think I could hold out, no matter how hard I tried."

"You don't have to hold out, and you don't have to try. Just quit trying and start trusting," Beau said. "Now, let me show you here from the Book of Thessalonians how you can be a part of that great Turnpike of Truth. I can show you in ten minutes how you can get out from under life's circumstances and get under the blood. You see, life is a matter of the Three R's."

"Reading . . . 'riting . . . and 'rithmetic?" asked J.B. naively.

"Nope," grinned Beau, smiling that J.B. was so ignorant of the Thessalonian Turnpike. "Recognizing, Repenting, and Receiving. First you recognize your lost condition. Then you repent of your sin, and then you can receive the gospel and be saved by the blood."

"I'd like to believe in the Book of *Thessalonicans*—" said J.B., seriously mispronouncing the word.

"Thessalonians! THESSALONIANS!" Beau corrected.

"Yes, but right now I've got more important things to consider."

"J.B., there are no more important things than to believe the Three R's and save your soul from an eternal devil's Hell. . . ."

That is how it went. Beau's concern expressed itself in cliches. He is deeply earnest about it all, however. J.B. appears anxious to be "under the blood." He seems earnest, too.

I must close. J.B. has just accepted an invitation to tonight's Conquest after all. What a rapturous turn of events!

Just as they are, they have come from the night,
Invading infinity, dwelling in light.
From the kingdom of graves and realms of the dead
They have turned to the Day Spring of Life.

Alleluia,
Valiant

# On the Way
to the
Conquest

WELL, HERE WE ARE IN the automobile on the way to the Conquest. I know I am still trying too hard, for I am too concerned with J.B.'s anxieties. Still, I believe that he is very near the most important decision of his life.

I gasp at human possibilities. J.B. has the possibility of grandeur we angels never can experience: reclamation. Can you imagine? Beginning existence as ordinary flesh and ending it in obvious love. Scuttlers taste forgiving grace, while we angels only know what it is like to be loved in foundational purity. Ah, to be lifted from dank materiality by the loving hand of the Lord High Command! I hope soon to enter into the full joy of my client.

When J.B. attended Grace Church, he was less impressed with their praise. Now I wonder whether it was because the number who gather in Grace Church is smaller than the Conquest crowd. Scuttlers themselves are prone to evaluate the success of religious meetings merely by the number in attendance. It is a shallow habit. J.B. must drop this assumption. His fascination with the mass assembly lies in his need for personal identity. There is truth in the human cliche: "A man is known by the company he keeps." J.B. feels bigger in big gospel meetings. Being a part of 30,000 sinners at once makes being a sinner seem less sinful. They have been publishing Conquest attendance in the daily papers. It excites J.B. to be part of such a large venture.

The success syndrome of Christian enterprises that fascinates J.B. bothers me. He watches Frankie Williams with all the adulation he would give a resurrected saint. In his misplaced esteem he again confuses "bigness" with "greatness," and "popularity" with "spirituality."

It disturbs me that J.B. has so little adulation for Grace Church. By contrast with the Conquest, Grace Church appears small and unimpressive. This is unfortunate, for much of the human dedication at Grace Church is beautiful. It has all that the Conquest offers plus a spiritual rapport that is warm and affirming. I cannot expect you to understand baseball. It amuses me only because it keeps guardians flying over a large grassy area to stay near their clients. They must feel as I do when J.B. and I are on the tennis court—a frenzied act of guardianship I must not try to describe.

I distract myself . . . where was I? . . . oh, yes . . . well. . . . Baseball teams are divided into leagues. Those that hold less interest are referred to as the Minors. Well, J.B. is giving the Conquest Major League esteem, and Grace Church, Minor. I regret that I am earthbound in my illustration. I hope mortal esteem for Williams does not blunt the esteem they ought to feel for Christ. Misplaced admiration thrives on Muddy-scuttle. Still, Frankie Williams seems worthy of the confidence placed in him. He is a man snared in the web of his calling. He does not covet prestige. He has strength without arrogance in spite of his Major League status. Whatever I might say of Williams, he does play a critical role in J.B.'s hoped-for reclamation. I trust that when Frankie Williams leaves this city, Grace Church will continue all that the Conquest began in Considine.

But neither Frankie Williams nor Grace Church shall determine this matter. I have become all the more aware that it is Christ who draws men to himself. The universal love of God designs the best circumstances to guide every person to life. I see what J.B. cannot see—that he is not alone in his struggle. He thinks that everything depends on himself. He thrashes like a new swimmer making a desperate crossing. Christ endured the agony of death for my client. It is Christ, I tell you, who has

erected a thousand barriers of love to keep J.B. from traveling his hapless way to nothingness. I thrill at the thoroughness of divine love. To end in Daystar's pit, J.B. must struggle over a hundred barricades of grace. Think of the obstacles God has already laid in J.B.'s path to self-destruction: Aunt Ida, MacDonald, Beau Ridley, Grace Church, Cassie, Frankie Williams, and even the biopsy. But Cassie is the key.

Cassie is preparing to attend a spiritual renewal weekend when the Conquest is over. She and many other singles will travel on chartered buses to a mountain retreat for extensive Bible study and prayer. As for Cassie and J.B., their relationship cannot maintain this distance much longer. They are clearly in love. Cassie consumes his thinking. Alphalite says Cassie has intense reciprocal feelings.

The last reckoning is desperate and close for my client. J.B. must come to know the Logos, and soon. Still, the ever-reaching love of God is constantly thwarted by J.B.'s pursuit of mere romance. Humans rarely seek higher affection if a lower one is accessible.

Human love is, indeed, powerful if only to humans. Nonetheless, I may have given such love a lower rating than it deserves. It is unfortunate that I lived so closely with the gluttonous sexual side of romance during my first assignment on this planet. In the case of J.B. and Cassie, their sweating, grunting, selfish indulgence may at last have risen from its muddy roots to become the very image of God's love.

What of J.B.'s love for Williams? Call it esteem, if you will. Still, J.B.'s reverence for the evangelist may be more natural than I should like to admit. Humans tend to admire those who assist the Logos in reclamation. I was aghast that Ridley approached my client with the Thessalonian Turnpike. Yet it accents the substance of the Logos' last human command, "Into all the world—preach the gospel to every creature"—those were his last words. So what if Beau Ridley is not very far advanced in the way he goes about it? He is being true to Christ's command even as he uses his zealous, mechanistic, and mundane cybernetics. And when Frankie Williams is no longer in Cleveland, I will then be glad that Beau is working with J.B. in any way.

> *Comes now the great and holy state,*
> *And promise beckons us to wait.*

Alleluia,
Valiant

The Triumph

HALLELUJAH! RELUCTANCE HAS BEEN SLAIN! J.B. has been set free from the bonds of Daystar! It happened at the Conquest on the last night that Frankie Williams was in town. It is difficult to tell of the soul-struggle J.B. encountered.

As he made his public commitment, all my fears of spurious identity were allayed. Neither the size of the crowd nor Frankie Williams was much in his mind at the time of his reclamation. Glorious truth! Wherever true reclamation occurs, it is always a highly individual matter. Although he stood before the Conquest crowd, it seemed to J.B. that he and the Logos were the only two in Cleveland.

His joy can hardly be described! He is filled with peace and a feeling of enlightenment. His whole being seems to have a quality of richness—a new wealth that derives from his spiritual inheritance. There are many aspects to this.

First, he has acquired the wonderful inwardness that is the inviolate principle of Upperton. This inwardness is not *sui generis*. He has created neither its being nor its value. It is the substance of an invasion that has flooded his life, through the narrowest opening of his will. He desired this inwardness only in little amounts, but it came in torrents. The flood has dumbfounded him with light. He willed it all, and yet there is so much more than he willed.

Joy is so innate to us that I can barely understand its impact, first discovered. These who have been born empty often come to fullness in a deluge of mood. Their joy makes visible the existence of our realm. It is not the only evidence of Christ that the planet sees, but it is most dynamic.

To be sure, new joy has an element of exhibitionism in it. J.B. sings constantly these days. His vocal quality is as poor as his spirit is rich. Thankfully, his musical expression is covert. He reserves it for himself and the angels. He sings in the shower— a common human tendency I do not claim to understand. But singing anywhere is new to my client since his joy came upon him. It is not sterile joy. He now has an interest in Bible reading that is spontaneous, and no longer motivated by his threatening memory of Aunt Ida. Further, he no longer resents Scripture for its long words of "begat" passages. Wondrously, he reads and has not been stopped once by the "begat" passages.

He is making a marked effort toward personal reform. He now questions himself about every form of indulgence that he once freely allowed. He is viewing gluttony and drunkenness, lust and jealousy from a new perspective. The accursed "girlie books" are all gone now . . . even those he considered the best. He has canceled a planned trip for rest and relaxation which was to include the loosest sort of activities. He no longer uses the name of the Lord High Command in Muddyscuttle phrases. But most impressive of all is a formidable new mental discipline with which he garrisons his thoughts.

It is spring, and even I am taken with the beauty of earth. The greens and blues of planets such as this have a charm all their own. There are still evidences of the fall of man all about . . . bits of rusted steel, candy wrappers, and decaying beverage cans. Yet a strong joy gathers new life from buds about to break into flowers. This feeling blankets the fields and hills. I wonder how this wondrous planet would have looked without Daystar's contamination. How foolish Adam was to blight his world for the slithering proposition of evil.

The world seems suddenly so new that I can scarcely believe I have been on the planet for years. I wish J.B. would go into the country alone to celebrate his new joy and leave me dumbfounded on the warm earth. Earth is not the pigsty I had first thought. Now, in the explosion of spring, I understand how our Beloved Logos felt. I know at last why God so loved this world that he permitted the humanization.

I must not give you the impression that J.B. is altogether changed. He is not ready for canonization. He is still struggling with his lower nature. He noticed Cassie yesterday during a less captivating moment of the sermon. Even in church his mind descended rapidly below his higher nature. He was almost engulfed in the same lust he experienced when they were living together. It was seething, if unexpressed. Yet he maintained a reverent look as a masquerade.

As I looked around, all the other Scuttlers in pew twenty-eight looked the same way, and I was hit by a cold chill. What ghastly indulgences lurked behind all those pious faces! Had I pores, I should have sweated.

Soon the pastor spoke a sharper thought, and J.B. left his fantasies and returned to his old sweet self, as they say down here. I was alarmed—his self was not so sweet after all. His hypocrisy was instant and stifling. He could entertain rank gluttony while appearing to feast on the adoration of the Logos.

His lust was intense and real. I did not imagine it. He experienced it! And all right in church! It has left me with a strange foreboding, and I cannot stay my fear. Are my hopes to be dashed by his permissive mind?

Further, while friends rejoice over his reclamation, I fear that Grace Church may dilute his zeal. He is being rushed all at once to join too many church organizations. He has been asked to join two choirs, two Sunday school classes, the bowling league, the men's club, the discussion team, and the Saturday Night Meet-a-Friend club. Should he try to join all these church groups, he will become busier than he is spiritual. He will be all legs and no heart in a short time. He has so far resisted the recruiters, but I don't know how long he can hold out.

I fear that this new fervor may be diverted to secondary allegiances. I shudder to think he might join so many good causes and yet miss the best.

Joy is here
For life has come
And death is speechless,
Ordered dumb.

Alleluia,
Valiant

In the Bus Terminal

A WEEK HAS PASSED SINCE J.B.'s reclamation, and I now find myself in a bus depot. As always I have my journal with me, including copies of this document for the Committee. I carry this file with me because of the certainty of my client's termination. But I must hurriedly conclude these papers, for the time is at hand. It is time to board the bus that J.B. must ride into foreverness.

May I tell you of my client's latest joy? He and Cassie have been exploring a tentative relationship. They are here with forty or more others waiting to board a motorbus for a trip they suppose will take them to a renewal center.

J.B. is unsuspecting. For him this is an opportunity for participating in a time of Bible study. Being with Cassie has doubled his joy. He is full of promises yet unspoken to both the Logos and to Cassie. J.B. and Cassie are sitting and talking quietly about the new meaning which is so abundant in their current relationship. Their new rapport has blotted out their past affair. It seems so sad! Now that they openly celebrate their relationship, it is over.

Now I can accept the great wisdom of the Committee. A divinity student would have been all wrong for me. At last I agree with my assignment. During J.B.'s struggle to become, I have arrived at a new plateau of angelic understanding. We have both been changed by the strange process of refining love.

I do love him. I know the High Command loves him, and we are in complete agreement. He is mine for only a few more hours. Shortly we shall both be back before the Chair. I anticipate the moment.

The chartered motorbus has pulled in and the passengers are called for. J.B. and Cassie are standing hand in hand. They are the joy of the Logos and could teach their world the glory of a good confession. Unfortunately, they are out of time. They would be grieved if they suspected they will never see Cleveland together again. It is not horror, but a delightful surprise that awaits them.

Excuse me that I've left this report so truncated. But I must go and watch these lovers safely across the chasm of mortality. They have run out of time. But no matter, they can get on without it now.

Summon the herald trumpets
Beneath the vast glass dome!
Love redefining death and love
Escorts her pilgrims home.

Alleluia,
Valiant

Afterword

ONE FRIDAY NIGHT IN APRIL, I was traveling through Cleveland, Ohio. I was to change buses after a short layover and continue to Buffalo, New York. As we pulled into the terminal, I noticed a chartered bus filled with men and women who appeared to be somewhat older than college age. Through the large windows of the bus I could see they were sitting in a random fashion, not in the customary heterosexual arrangement of young marrieds. I assumed, therefore, that they were singles departing on some lark. I could not immediately think of the nature of their outing since it was too late for the ski season and too early for summer vacations.

One couple near the back window of the bus was strumming guitars and singing. As a pastor I have seen enough of guitars and young folk, and I suddenly realized it was a religious retreat in its formative stages.

Our buses passed slowly. The one on which I rode pulled into the gate that the charter had vacated. This turned out to be the most timely of departures and arrivals. I was shortly to make an amazing discovery.

I found myself sitting in the terminal with my briefcase under my seat. I leaned back against the sweater that I had removed. I was uncomfortably warm and feeling a touch of nausea which I attributed to the irregular motion of the bus in the heavy city traffic.

While waiting for the bus to Buffalo, I sat absent-mindedly running my hand over the empty seat next to the one I occupied. In this distracted activity my fingers fell upon a sticky surface. I thought it to be cola accidently spilled by a clumsy child probably as impatient as I to board a bus.

I instinctively recoiled. Something from the seat clung to my finger tips. The stickiness was not a beverage slick as I had thought, but a piece of semi-adhesive cellophane the size of typing paper, except much thinner. When I held the transparency to the light, I could see that it was not entirely clear. It contained some characters nearly impossible to read. The tiny "glyphs" appeared to be a faded form of handwriting. I squinted in a vain attempt to make the queer etchings yield words, or even a single recognizable letter. They would not.

As I placed my hand upon the empty seat again, the sticky sensation recurred. Once more I drew back, and just as surely had lifted a second piece of this clear film bearing the same faint, unintelligible characters. I placed this second transparency behind the first and reached again to the empty seat. Another sheet adhered. Some thirty times I repeated the procedure until I had lifted and stacked everything that the seat contained. I arranged the sheets in exactly the order that I had retrieved them. When my hand finally fell on naked wood, I felt somehow cheated that the strange adventure was over.

My next activity must have appeared strange to others in the terminal. I rose and checked my own seat to be sure there were no sheets there. I moved along the row of empty chairs until I came to one occupied by a rather portly gentleman. He peered at me over the top of his newspaper in a way that unnerved me and halted my search.

I did not fold the sheets, but put them directly into my attache case, planning to examine them later. As I placed them in the case, I took two aspirin from it and swallowed them, hoping to alleviate a headache that had grown to a dull throb during my stay in the terminal.

My bus was called at last. I grabbed my sweater and attache case and walked to the gate. I boarded the bus still feeling nausea. My condition worsened. I began to feel alternately chills and fever. The long ride to Buffalo became one of the most arduous trips of my life.

Several times on the bus I fell asleep in a deep slumber that resembled a coma. In brief moments of consciousness I feared that I might be experiencing some sort of seizures. In spasms of unconsciousness it seemed I heard the wing-beats of some very large bird. In conscious moments I attributed these strange flutterings to the delirium of my fever.

I prayed to be free of the sickness. But neither aspirin nor prayer offered deliverance. Several times I thought of asking the driver to stop to see if he might arrange my transportation to the nearest hospital. But usually, by breathing deeply, I could feel some relief. In these better moments I felt embarrassed that I had thought myself to be sick at all.

Finally I arrived in Buffalo, took a cab to my hotel, and checked in. Once in my room, I turned down my bed. I wanted to collapse immediately into deep healing sleep. However, my mind turned again to those mysterious sheets in my briefcase. My curiosity was greater than my weariness, so I unsnapped the latches.

The sticky sheets were still there. While they had not grown thicker, they were becoming more opaque. I was delighted to see that the characters which had been too dim to read grew more distinct as the papers lost their transparency. Most of all, I was relieved to see that they were written in English. I could now actually make out words and sentences. I knew if their legibility continued to improve, they would be quite readable by morning.

But again illness and fatigue overwhelmed me. I put the sheets back in the case and went to sleep. During the night I experienced more spells of fever accompanied by the sensation of audible but invisible flutterings.

By morning the illness was gone. I awoke with a start when the events of the previous day flooded into my consciousness. Suddenly and brilliantly the sun invaded my room.

I leaped from bed and grabbed my case. Eagerly I tore it open and discovered the strange sheets were still there. The crisp English sentences were bright, sharp, and exquisitely written on a kind of gossamer stationery.

I do not need to comment on the contents of the strange papers, for they formed the document that has become this book. I sensed in my first hurried reading that the material was in the process of decay even as I set about the task of copying it. What I thought I had, I now knew I was about to lose. I grabbed a pad and a pen and began the transcription in a race against time. I was determined that it be a race I would not lose.

I neared the end of my work twenty-four hours later. As I copied the last few pages, they were hard to read, and some of the text was obscure. The characters faded. The sheets grew again transparent and soon were invisible. Shortly even the desk where I had last laid them would not yield a tactile smudge. It was as though they had been absorbed into the wood and were gone.

All that remains from those curious pages is my handwritten copy. It is my hope that the reality of the elusive original will affirm the existence of a world which parallels our own.

The material herein contained was not intended for publication—at least on this planet. I believe I have acted properly, however, in releasing this manuscript. If not, I alone bear the responsibility. I have changed the names of the mortals involved. The other names appear exactly as I found them.

Calvin Miller
Omaha, Nebraska

Other Books of Interest
from Servant Books

Cry Freedom
The Story of Lida Vashchenko and Her
Remarkable Escape from Soviet Russia
by Lida Vashchenko

One of the Siberian Seven shares the tragedy and the triumph
of life as a Christian in Soviet Russia. The powerful and
dramatic true story of a family's suffering and final escape.
$5.95

Chasing the Dragon
by Jackie Pullinger with Andrew Quike

The true story of how one woman's faith resulted in the
conversion of hundreds of drug addicts, prositutes, and
hardened criminals in Hong Kong's infamous Walled City.
$4.50

Available at your Christian bookstore or from:
**Servant Publications • Dept. 209 • P.O. Box 7455
Ann Arbor, Michigan 48107**
Please include payment plus $.75 per book
for postage and handling.
*Send for our FREE catalog of Christian
books, music, and cassettes.*